MW01223722

RALPH MATHEKGA

WHEN ZUMA GOES

Tafelberg

Tafelberg
An imprint of NB Publishers, a Division of Media24 Boeke (Pty) Ltd
40 Heerengracht, Cape Town
www.tafelberg.com
Text © Ralph Mathekga (2016)

All rights reserved.
No part of this book may be reproduced or transmitted in any form
or by any electronic or mechanical means, including photocopying and
recording, or by any information storage or retrieval system,
without written permission from the publisher.

Cover design: Nudge Studio
Book design: Nazli Jacobs
Editing: Alfred LeMaitre
Proofreading: Sean Fraser
Index: Sanet le Roux

Printed and bound by Creda Communications,
Eliot Avenue, Epping II, Cape Town

First edition, first impression 2016

ISBN: 978-0-624-08067-1
Epub: 978-0-624-08068-8
Mobi: 978-0-624-08069-5

This book is dedicated to
my parents, Solomon and Constance Mathekga,
for always encouraging me to make my case
whenever I feel I have a case to make.

Contents

List of abbreviations

Amcu Association of Mineworkers and Construction Union
ANC African National Congress
APRM African Peer Review Mechanism
AU African Union

BEE Black Economic Empowerment

CIA Central Intelligence Agency
Cope Congress of the People
Cosas Congress of South African Students
Cosatu Congress of South African Trade Unions

DA Democratic Alliance
DRC Democratic Republic of Congo

EFF Economic Freedom Fighters

GDP gross domestic product
Gear Growth, Employment and Redistribution

Icasa Independent Communications Authority of South Africa
ICC International Criminal Court

JCPS Justice, Crime Prevention and Security
JSC Judicial Service Commission

MK Umkhonto we Sizwe
MTSF Medium Term Strategic Framework
NDP National Development Plan
NDPP National Director of Public Prosecutions
NEC National Executive Committee
NIA National Intelligence Agency
NPA National Prosecuting Authority
NPC National Planning Commission
NUM National Union of Mineworkers
Numsa National Union of Metalworkers of South Africa

PAC Pan Africanist Congress
PIC Public Investment Corporation
Prasa Passenger Rail Agency of South Africa

SAA South African Airways
SABC South African Broadcasting Corporation
SACP South African Communist Party
SAHRC South African Human Rights Commission
SARS South African Revenue Service

UDM United Democratic Movement

Foreword by Justice Malala

The past and the present are not contested. With the 1994 demo-cratic breakthrough we started off relatively well and have now reached a cul-de-sac. The real question is this: what now? What does the future hold? It would seem that in the hurly-burly of our present political impasse we have forgotten how to raise our eyes to the future and begin to interrogate what the South Africa of our children will look like.

South African political discourse has been in the grip of the Jacob Zuma phenomenon since May 2005, when he was fired by then president Thabo Mbeki. We have been in the grip of the 'Zunami', the politics of performance instead of policy, the rise of populism with nary a thought of the actual work of govern-ment and the empowerment of people.

Zuma has become the central figure of our politics. His personal and political scandals are numerous; his gaffes are legendary; his grip on power absolute; his survival skills a thing of wonder. His political demise has been predicted thousands of times by pundits across the globe. His continued presence proves them all wrong.

The man has become a mirage, his face on the front pages of newspapers and the headlines of television news bulletins, yet he is still a closed book to the people he leads. To the citizens of South Africa, the question 'Who is Jacob Zuma?' still resonates.

We may never really know. What Ralph Mathekga aims to

achieve is to take the political football we are toying with and yank us towards the real game: our future needs to be addressed now, and addressed seriously.

This is because that future is being written now. As the South African political landscape unfolds, serious damage is being done to the key to our future: the institutions of democracy. Cast your eye to the courts, which have been labelled 'reactionary' and 'counter-revolutionary'. The Zuma administration chose to disobey a court order ruling that South Africa should respect its international obligations by arresting the Sudanese strongman, Omar al-Bashir, and sending him to face trial in the International Criminal Court (ICC).

Cast your eye over the Hawks, the supposedly independent crime-fighting unit that was set up to investigate high-profile serious crimes. The Hawks replaced the much-admired Scorpions, the independent unit that investigated and put together the 783 counts of fraud, racketeering and corruption that Zuma has evaded since 2005. The Hawks are now led by an apartheid-era policeman who was found by the Pretoria High Court to have lied under oath.

There are many other examples. Remember that Zuma survived an impeachment vote in April 2016 after the Constitutional Court said he failed in his duty to uphold, defend and protect the Constitution by ignoring the Public Protector's recommendation that he repay some of the R246 million in state funds spent on renovating his home.

Then think about his effect on the respect and integrity of state institutions. In December 2015, he did untold damage to the currency and the National Treasury when he fired the respected Finance minister, Nhlanhla Nene, and replaced him with a hapless unknown junior MP. Trust built up over years in the stability

of South Africa's financial institutions evaporated, and that mistrust remains among domestic and international investors.

This is what we know. This is what we have seen happen before
our eyes. So what do the next ten years look like? How do we
get on an upward trajectory? For anyone interested in the future
of South Africa, this is the gaping hole in our political discourse.
Our conversation has nothing concrete that shows us the damage
wrought by the Zuma years and how we fix the problems the next
generation is saddled with.

Ralph Mathekga has become one of South Africa's most respected political analysts because he is obsessed with the future. In the
Cold War years, he would have been one of the sages of the South
African political landscape, for very few people can read our tea
leaves as astutely and as effectively as he does. He gets the future
right by reading the past and present correctly.

In this valuable book, Mathekga casts his eye forwards and
begins to fill the void at the heart of our political discourse: how
do we fix the damage of the Zuma years? What do those who will
follow us need to do to set the country on what scenario planner
Clem Sunter characterises as the high road to a brighter future?

The questions are tough and the answers are not easy to find.
However, we, as a nation, cannot afford to look away and fiddle
as our roof burns. We have to look the questions in the eye – hard.
We have to do some very serious introspection.

Mathekga takes a hard look at our past, present and future, and,
in his usual, unflinching style, takes our hand and begins to show
us the path out of our current quagmire. This is an urgent and
necessary book.

Justice Malala
Johannesburg, August 2016

Prologue

The good analyst does not take sides; it is not his duty to judge, for he is obliged to explain and provide a wider perspective. In order to explain developments and the actors who are at the forefront of developments, all of the actors should be accorded the same level of respect. Some actors may seem too shallow and lacking in sophistication to merit focused analysis. But it is the duty of an analyst to explain how these actors fit into the greater scheme of things.

History teaches us that people who have a major impact on the world are sometimes initially dismissed as lacking in sophistication and/or clear goals. But once that person finds himself in the middle of destruction, or in the driver's seat of a massive campaign to change the world, the spotlight falls on them while people wonder how that person managed to get into such a position of power. That is when the pundits try to make sense of that political actor's story, and try to understand why he was ignored in the first place. Years ago, Jacob Zuma was dismissed by many as a pariah, a man with no formal education and therefore incapable of committing to anything that could have an impact on society. Yet he will go down in history as one of the most controversial presidents in South African history, a man whose methods have been misunderstood and often oversimplified.

In this book, I aim to avoid simplifying Zuma. I want to understand the logic of his methods, and how that logic is reflected in his party, the African National Congress (ANC), and in society in general. There is a sense that the ANC would prefer to move away from the Zuma years, to write off its losses, and to completely extricate itself from the man. But this will not explain how the party produced Zuma, and what his impact has been on the party. If indeed the ANC were allowed to conveniently turn the page on Zuma, the nation would be left to ask whether another Zuma might eventually emerge within the ANC. It is only through a searching analysis of how Zuma emerged within the ANC in particular, and in South Africa in general, that we can come to a full understanding of what might lie ahead.

Perhaps Zuma is not an outlier; perhaps he is a necessary stage in the development of our country. He represents a particular stage in the development of the system. In order to understand what he represents, he should be looked at in comparison, and it has to be a fair comparison. There should be no judgement in carrying out this analysis. Whether one is right or wrong, in trying to understand what will happen when Zuma goes, it is important to start from the point of view that he is a product of South African society. One way or another, South Africa has to account for how Zuma emerged from within the ANC, and from within our society. This exercise is a necessary step in attempting to understand what will happen when Zuma goes. The problem might not be Zuma himself; the problem might be the common sense of the nation that trusted him to lead. The question is: can this nation be trusted not to repeat the same mistake?

ONE

~~~

The rise of the 'man of the people'

The ascension of Jacob Zuma to the presidency of the African National Congress (ANC) is a phenomenon that continues to be seen as an exception to the rule. The explanations for Zuma's triumph against the odds verge on the miraculous. Just how those odds were stacked against him makes for an interesting story. And in the nation's collective psyche, Zuma stands as a lone hero who triumphed against a legion of enemies. I was not entirely surprised by Jacob Zuma's ascension, however; the soil was fertile for the appearance of such a leader. More than that, I believe that if Jacob Zuma did not exist, the populists would have invented him.

The key to how Zuma made it to the ANC presidency, and then became president of the country, lies in understanding the legacy of former president Thabo Mbeki, and in the ongoing evolution of the ANC as a political party. If we look closely at Mbeki's administration style, particularly the way in which the state started to relate to citizens and political parties, it becomes clear that a gap was created between the party and the institutions of government. And this gap conveniently accommodated the emerging Jacob Zuma cult. Zuma was packaged as an alternative to Mbeki; however, a closer look suggests that Jacob Zuma actually represents a particular way in which citizens are trying to relate to the people in power. And it is the antithesis of Thabo Mbeki's approach to modernising the state and his relations with citizens. The idea of Zuma as an alternative was created in an attempt to normalise the frosty relationship between citizens and the formal institutions of government.

In 2006, during the personal legal woes that confronted Jacob Zuma after he was fired as deputy president of the country,[1] I presented a paper at the third biennial conference of the South African Political Studies Association, held at the University of the Western Cape (UWC). The paper was titled 'The ANC Leadership Crisis and the Age of Populism in Post-apartheid South Africa'. At the time, Zuma's problems with the ANC appeared to be a straightforward case of an individual member of the party who had made a mistake by associating with an unsavoury character, namely, Schabir Shaik. Mbeki dealt with the problem by removing Zuma from government. That proved to be the beginning and not the end of the problem.

Zuma was facing corruption charges, which were subsequently followed by rape charges.[2] Many South Africans believed this was the end of Zuma's political career. But Zuma's personal troubles distracted everyone's attention from the political circumstances that reigned within the ANC and the country at that time. My argument was that the ANC was shifting towards a populist direction, and the country – at that time – was willing to embrace such a shift. This was, in my view, a moment when the party was searching for a political figurehead with whom people could identify, someone who represented a leadership style different from that of the autocratic Thabo Mbeki. This populist wave was not triggered or created by Jacob Zuma, but he would ride the wave to secure

---

1   Political Bureau, 'Zuma axed', Independent Online, 14 June 2005. Available at www.iol.co.za. Accessed on 25 July 2016.
2   Jenni Evans and Riaan Wolmarans, 'Timeline of Jacob Zuma rape trial', *Mail & Guardian*, 21 March 2016. Available at mg.co.za. Accessed on 25 July 2016.

the presidency of the ANC and that of the country, and would later abandon the populist ticket once he became president, surrounding himself with a few trusted friends.

At the time, I argued that recent developments in the South African political landscape had raised questions about the political leadership emerging in the country – and only just a little over a decade after apartheid had ended. Since it came to power in 1994, the ruling ANC had largely defined the leadership fabric in the country, with its political project grounded on a moral appeal derived from the party's role as a leader of both the liberation movement and the process of transformation. Recent events in South Africa, though, had left the ruling party on the defensive, and the ANC found it necessary to explain itself in terms of the leadership that it stood for. The need for introspection on the part of the ANC seems to have emerged after the dismissal of Jacob Zuma as deputy president in June 2005, due to his alleged involvement in corruption. Zuma was able to mobilise popular support among different ANC structures and within the trade unions, where the populist agenda was increasingly seen as an alternative to Mbeki's style of leadership.

That was how I understood the political environment in which Jacob Zuma emerged, and how that environment rejected Thabo Mbeki. For me, it has never been about two individuals, but rather about how society and institutions shape their fate. Of course, their responses to circumstances would shape the particular way that Mbeki would exit and Zuma would enter South Africa's political leadership. But personally, the two men had nothing to do with the main point, which was that it was becoming necessary for one form of leadership to take over from the other. At the time this explanation made sense to me. Eventually the same fate that troubled Mbeki would also trouble Zuma. The main difference

between the two leaders in how they dealt with challenges within the party and society is that the one was able to learn from the
mistakes of the other: Zuma had the privilege of learning from
Mbeki's mistakes. This explains why Zuma would hold on to power
despite the numerous major problems he would encounter. Mbeki, on the other hand, had to write the script from scratch, and
he got it wrong.

The framing of the conflict between Zuma and Mbeki is better
understood in terms of both leadership style and expectations
from the broader society and the party. When his supporters
put Zuma forward as an alternative to Mbeki, the case was made
that Zuma had a more open and consultative leadership approach.[3]
This comparison is rather inadequate, because, by that time, Zuma
had not occupied any position where his leadership style might
have revealed itself. In fact, his leadership style could only be traced
back to his role within the exiled ANC during the liberation struggle as the head of counter-intelligence and various secret operations.[4] Prior to his 1999 appointment as deputy president of the
country, he served as Member of the Executive Council (MEC)
for Economic Affairs in the province of KwaZulu-Natal. A minor
provincial appointment such as this does not license one to show
the sort of leadership that would warrant comparison with a sitting president.

In addition, the position of deputy president is effectively a
ceremonial one, unless the individual in that position is so driven
that he or she attempts to make something out of it. The deputy's

---

3   *The Economist*, 'Voting for the people's man', 16 April 2009. Available at
    www.economist.com. Accessed on 14 May 2015.
4   Patrick Laurence, 'Jacob Zuma and Imbokodo', politicsweb, 3 March 2009.
    Available at www.politicsweb.co.za. Accessed on 25 July 2016.

actual responsibilities largely involve presiding over the reburial of struggle heroes' remains, attending the funerals of dignitaries and possibly also convening not-so-interesting inter-ministerial committees, which usually fall apart after a few meetings. It is difficult, if not impossible, to recognise a leadership style from someone in this position, which made it convenient to compare Zuma's virtually non-existent leadership style with Mbeki's tight grip on power.

By then Mbeki's leadership style had become apparent over the years, largely in the way he arranged state institutions. In 2000, in a play on Brian Pottinger's book about PW Botha, *The Imperial Presidency*, political scientist Sean Jacobs[5] was the first to describe Mbeki's leadership style[6] as an 'imperial presidency'. Mbeki has subsequently written a series of letters attempting to dismiss the idea that he was obsessed with power. At least the former president is aware of the perception that he was aloof.

The idea that Mbeki's administration was an 'imperial presidency' was derived from the way he organised the state bureaucracy. This, in turn, influenced how his political party (the ANC) and ordinary citizens would relate to the state. Assertions were made that Mbeki was a centrist, and that he preferred to concentrate power in a few government institutions that he could personally control. I bought into this idea at first. However, as I began to think it through back in 2006, it became clear that before Mbeki took over as president, following the collapse of the apartheid regime, South Africa had no coherent state bureaucracy. Under apartheid, South Africa had a highly centralised state system aimed

5   Currently Assistant Professor of International Affairs at the New School for Social Research in New York.

6   Sean Jacobs, 'An imperial presidency or an organized one?', *Business Day*, 17 February 2000.

at ensuring stability in the country, while pushing against any attempts to delegitimise the regime. The organisation of society centred on the use of the security apparatus, and government did not see itself as obligated to account to citizens. That configuration did not allow for the creation of the type of bureaucracy based on democratic principles, including the separation of powers between the executive, the judiciary and the legislature. Mbeki's attempt to build a modern bureaucracy was the first concerted effort after apartheid.

President Nelson Mandela had attempted to lay the foundations for a state bureaucracy. But it was Mbeki who consolidated the bureaucracy and gave it a recognisable shape. His approach was not perfect, but it laid a solid basis for what we have today. Before I explain how Mbeki did that, it is important to stress the main point of this analysis: the manner in which Mbeki organised the state bureaucracy produced a situation where his own party grew more and more discontented. They felt restricted in their relations with the state, and this attitude gave rise to the idea that Mbeki was 'aloof' and not in touch with the people. This image was grafted onto his personality and his leadership style, and then compared with that of a man who had not yet really developed a leadership style – Jacob Zuma.

Zuma would ultimately encounter problems in crafting his own leadership style because it had already been imagined and assigned to him – as the opposite of Mbeki's leadership approach. But Mbeki's own tendency to be overzealous got the better of him when he dreamed of a third term as president of the ANC.[7] That mistake cemented the legend of his aloofness and gave it a life of

7   James Myburgh, 'Thabo Mbeki and the "third term" issue', Moneyweb, 21 May 2007. Available at www.moneyweb.co.za. Accessed on 25 July 2016.

its own. No matter how many letters he would write to explain himself, they only drove home the idea that he was aloof.[8]

And concerns were emerging in the ANC that Mbeki was going his own way, without sufficient approval from Luthuli House, the party's headquarters in Johannesburg. At the time, it could be said that most ANC members and South African voters did not yet fathom the idea that a political party and the state are two different things. The party chooses ministers and officials to serve in government, and this may give the impression that the party *is* the state.

This problem often rears its head in Africa, where political parties in power operate under the illusion that they are the state, and thus the owners of state resources. A good example is Kenya under the leadership of Daniel arap Moi, who became president in 1978. It was only when Moi's party, the Kenya African National Union (Kanu), lost power in 2002 that the country realised it had been using government offices and resources to carry out party activities. This makes a strong case for the complete separation of government from the ruling party. But any African leader who tries to draw a line between the state and a political party will have to confront a political culture that seems to be well entrenched – and sees no need for such separation. I suppose one of the problems Mbeki encountered was that of separating the party from the state, which led to his falling-out with the party, and eventually to his removal from office before the end of his presidential term.

The distinction between a ruling party and the state is a key principle when it comes to understanding the politics of a post-liberation country such as South Africa. The state is like a plane full of passengers (the nation), who appoint an aircrew and cabin

8   Matuma Letsoalo, 'Jeremy Cronin hits back at Thabo Mbeki', *Mail & Guardian*, 21 January 2016. Available at mg.co.za. Accessed on 25 July 2016.

attendants (the ruling party) to fly them wherever they want to go. The crew do *not* own the aircraft; the passengers employ them. If the flights are smooth, their contracts might be renewed; too many bumpy landings and they'll be voted out – unless the crew hijacks the plane, of course, which provides a Zimbabwean flavour!

Thabo Mbeki angered many provincial ANC bigwigs when he decided to appoint the premiers of provinces directly, without following the party line of deployment.[9] According to party tradition, the ANC provincial chair is naturally in line to become provincial premier. The argument for this approach would be that, as the president of the country and the head of the executive branch of government, the president has the right to select whoever within the party he or she thinks would best implement the government's mandate. One of the administrative privileges of being the boss should be the ability to select your team, outside party constraints. It is only where the ruling party is not in charge, such as in the Western Cape province, that the president forfeits the chance to appoint a premier.

Thabo Mbeki was criticised for what I believe was an attempt to modernise the post-apartheid bureaucracy. In his own party there were discontented mumbles aplenty, including the accusation that Mbeki focused too much on international affairs and the so-called African agenda. It was said that he was not distributing the resources of the state in accordance with how the party preferred. In cruder terms, some critics said Mbeki was not pushing the 'party mandate', as he was obsessed with a Eurocentric version of how the state ought to be. It was whispered that Mbeki's demeanour was that of a snobbish English gentleman, who dealt with his comrades in an 'un-ANC' manner. So Mbeki's bureau-

---

9   William Gumede, *Thabo Mbeki and the Battle for the Soul of the ANC*. Cape Town: Zebra Press, 2007.

cratic reorganisation of the state was simply branded as coming from his personal obsession with power. This, in my view, is not entirely correct. Even under Jacob Zuma, there has been further consolidation of bureaucracy, and Zuma has not been accused of doing this to increase his power base. This is because Zuma was not suspected of being capable of harbouring sentiments to create and hold on to a power base. The perception that Zuma was a 'man of the people' also implied he was not the type of politician who is really interested in power politics. Zuma's experience in government, however, dispels the naive belief that he is only interested in singing and dancing. Like any politician, he indeed has an interest in latching on to and consolidating political power. What is even more notable about Zuma is that he is willing to trade political power for material benefits, as evidenced by the material enrichment of his children and family during his presidency.

Mbeki, on the other hand, steadfastly built the capacity of the state. In order to implement the complex macroeconomic policy that South Africa adopted after the collapse of apartheid, the state needed to be capable and the bureaucracy needed to be in place. This was achieved under Mbeki, notably in the strength of the National Treasury under Finance minister Trevor Manuel. While the National Treasury's role, responsibilities and areas of function are well provided for in the Constitution, Mbeki protected its financial management system against populist demands for relaxed fiscal targets.[10] Mbeki also protected the South African Reserve Bank's monetary policy, particularly the inflation targeting practice that has come under severe attack by the Congress of South African Trade Unions (Cosatu) and some within the ANC.

---

10 *Mail & Guardian*, 'A klap for government policy', 19 May 2008. Available at mg.co.za. Accessed on 25 July 2016.

The protection of such institutions from populist and party on-slaught represents further consolidation of bureaucracy in South Africa. But the ANC had yet to learn the lesson that you cannot just spend money as you wish. The idea had not sunk in that you cannot run a deficit to fund policies that you think are important. Fiscal discipline, proper fiscal management and the idea of 'fiscal reality' are usually seen as convenient ways of blocking the imple-mentation of progressive policies in newly liberated countries. The absence of these traits in a system usually indicates a poor level of bureaucratic development.

The operation of the Reserve Bank under its governor, Tito Mbo-weni, also showed further consolidation of state bureaucracy. The idea of inflation targeting, which necessarily requires the constant monitoring of the currency and subsequent protection of its value, came under attack as part of the anti-Mbeki crusade. Critics said that reining in inflation clashed with the nation's need for rapid industrial development. Cosatu has always maintained that infla-tion targeting keeps the value of the rand too high, and that the cost of production in local industries is therefore unsustainable. For Cosatu, economic policy – understood in terms of the need to accelerate expenditure and create jobs – should not be constrained. Together with the South African Communist Party (SACP), Cosatu argued that monetary policy should be subjected to the demands for rapid economic growth. In crude terms, Cosatu wants to spend at all costs, in the belief that growth will regulate inflation naturally, not deliberately, as the Reserve Bank has been doing. The attack against this approach intensified under Mbeki, causing headaches for Mboweni.[11]

Mboweni fended off calls to do away with inflation targeting

---

11 Nic Borain, 'The Spirit of Polokwane', 24 July 2009. Available at nicborain. wordpress.com. Accessed on 7 May 2015.

up until his departure from the Reserve Bank in 2009. His ability
to repel such calls was based on Mbeki's belief in the central bank
as part of his bureaucracy, and his devotion to the idea of an
independent central bank that would not be easily swayed by the
political mood of the day. Mboweni's retirement as the head of
the Reserve Bank was interpreted as the end of the inflation targeting policy. In a deeper sense, Mboweni's retirement presented
an opportunity to tinker with the bureaucracy that had kept South
Africa on a recovering fiscal path, with a stable currency and a
relatively low debt-to-GDP ratio. This bureaucracy also ensured
a low deficit, despite rising government spending on social security grants.

I am in no way of the opinion that Thabo Mbeki was a perfect
leader. There are numerous areas where he could have and should
have done better. Among the black spots on his presidency was
his approach to HIV/Aids. There are some in South Africa who
have called for him to be hauled before the International Criminal
Court at The Hague to be tried for crimes against humanity because of his stance on HIV/Aids. While this would be an extreme
measure, Mbeki certainly undermined the fight against HIV/Aids.
Further, the manner in which Mbeki handled calls for an arms
deal inquiry before he left office in September 2008 also showed
concern with saving the name of the party instead of allowing the
pursuit of justice. Mbeki relinquished power while maintaining
steadfastly that there was no need for a broader inquiry on the
arms deal. He maintained that those who had evidence of wrongdoing relating to the arms deal should present it to the law enforcement authorities.[12] Mbeki not only failed to initiate a full-scale

---

12 Thulani Gqirana, 'Some determined to prove Mandela's government was
   corrupt – Mbeki', News24, 25 April 2016. Available at www.news24.com.
   Accessed on 14 July 2016.

investigation into the arms deal, he also frustrated any meaningful inquiry. Jacob Zuma ultimately instituted the Seriti Commission to re-examine the arms deal. Zuma's commission arrived at
the same results as Mbeki, that there was nothing untoward about
the controversial deal, despite the conviction of former ANC chief
whip Tony Yengeni for impropriety relating to the deal[13] Perhaps
the only belief that Mbeki and Zuma share is the conviction that
there was no corruption relating to the arms deal.

   All of these failings, and others, do not detract from the fact
that Mbeki did a sterling job in consolidating state bureaucracy, a
bureaucracy that is the envy of many countries on the continent
and elsewhere. But with this process came unintended consequences, which created fertile ground for Jacob Zuma to emerge as an
alternative to Mbeki. The latter's attempt to clinch a third term
as the president of the party made Zuma even more attractive as
a leader.

   On a more complex level, it is difficult to build a modern bureaucracy in a situation where the majority of the people are still
desperately poor. If attempts are made to build a modern Western-
style state bureaucracy amid gross inequality and disturbing poverty levels,[14] that bureaucracy will be seen as attempting to shield
the state from the influence of the voters, particularly the economically destitute voters who need direct contact with the state as a
distributor of opportunities and resources. It has been argued con-
vincingly that poor countries will most likely not be able to sustain

13 Christopher Munnion, 'ANC chief whip on corruption charges', *The Tele-
    graph*, 4 October 2001. Available at www.telegraph.co.uk. Accessed on
    10 April 2016.
14 Haroon Bhorat, 'Is South Africa the most unequal society in the world?',
    Mail & Guardian, 30 September 2015. Available at mg.co.za. Accessed on
    17 February 2016.

democracy.[15] This is because of the burden of poverty and inequality on democracy. In a country where the majority of citizens
are poor, they would demand rapid response from democratic
institutions. This also means that they would find government
bureaucracy to be inaccessible; hence they will be more willing to
turn away from democracy.

This impasse, which commonly affects newer democracies,
often results in difficulties where the founding political party has
to transform itself from dispensing the rhetoric of serving the
people and bringing government to the people to being a modern
party functioning within the limits of a full-fledged bureaucracy.
By its nature, bureaucracy requires delegation, and essentially lacks
the direct point of contact that newly liberated citizens often yearn
for. Bureaucracy and the politics of representation will always be
alienating for citizens such as South Africans, the majority of whom
have been distant from government except when it policed their
affairs under apartheid.

As a founding party of South Africa's democratic dispensation,
the ANC has confronted this challenge in an interesting way. The
party naturally became alienated from the general populace, as it
presided over a bureaucratic and institutional framework requiring
that those in government were not in direct contact with voters.
This has resulted in the ANC finding it difficult to manage its own
transition from being a mass-based liberation movement to a
political party in charge of the modern state.

The ANC *is* finding it difficult to manage the transition. The
party *is* being forced to transform from a rhetorical mass political

15 Adam Przeworski, 'Democracy and economic development', in Edward D
Mansfield and Richard Sisson (eds), *Political Science and the Public Interest*.
Columbus: Ohio State University Press, 2004. Available at politics.as.nyu.
edu. Accessed on 25 July 2016.

movement to a modern political party. And the ANC in power *is* in charge of state resources – and responsible for those who might not even have voted for it. The pace and tenacity with which state bureaucracy intensified under Mbeki's two terms as president made it increasingly uncomfortable for the party to live up to the challenges of the day. The ANC naturally felt left out of state affairs during Mbeki's term, which widened the gap between the ANC and government. An opportunity existed for the emergence of a leadership that would bring government back under the party's thumb. The floor was open to calls for populism, which rested on a listening leader who would not only respond more to the party's demands on government, but was also expected to tame government and subject its functioning to the party's whims.

It did not take much effort to brand the consolidation of state bureaucracy as a Thabo Mbeki project. The idea of 'anyone but Mbeki' emerged, notably mobilised by Cosatu and the SACP, the two formations that did not enjoy privilege in accessing the state machinery, including the ANC leadership in government. The practical implication of a stronger and solid bureaucracy in a modern democracy is that it usually reduces the influence of labour on state policy. Cosatu and the SACP, being the bastions of organised labour, were not given sufficient space during the consolidation of bureaucracy under Mbeki. So it was Cosatu and the SACP that attempted a reformulation of the anti-bureaucracy stance as an alternative to Mbeki's leadership. Clumsily yet successfully, they mobilised the call for Zuma to emerge as a leader who would restore the position of the party in relation to the state – a leader who would effectively bring government back to the people.

Conveniently, Jacob Zuma was packaged as a victim of the excessive manipulation of state apparatus against an individual who connected with the people. Zuma was expected not to intensify the bureaucratisation of the state and its institutions, but to roll it back and customise it in a way that the broader 'masses', who brought him to power, would have a say in how government functions. The idea of an alternative gained momentum to the extent where it was only defined in relation to what it was not, and not what it actually entailed. It was a matter of a quick political machination to occupy the political space that was making itself readily available.

When Jacob Zuma emerged as an alternative to Mbeki, no efforts were made to demonstrate what he actually stood for. The focus was largely on what he would not be – and he would not be Mbeki. By then it was my strong belief that 'if Jacob Zuma did not exist, the populists would have invented him'. His emergence as the alternative had little to do with personal acumen. Instead he was framed in an idealist manner.

The reality has been that the populist euphoria that brought Zuma to power could not sustain him once he reached the Union Buildings. As president, he had to implement certain decisions that affirmed state bureaucracy, just as Mbeki had done. The main difference between Zuma and Mbeki in relation to the bureaucracy is that Mbeki played a fundamental role in engineering the state bureaucracy and paid a price for this, while Zuma only had to maintain and strengthen the bureaucracy that was already in place, and to use it carefully to ensure his political survival.

While Zuma may differ with Mbeki in terms of rhetoric, the two men's actions as statesmen and presidents follow the familiar bureaucratic trail constructed by Mbeki. The lesson from Zuma's rise to power is that populism is good when it comes to replacing leaders, but not in sustaining leadership. Having come to power by surfing the populist wave, Zuma could not run the state by the same means. Further, by having to follow the bureaucracy of government, Zuma found himself in a situation where he could not claim to balance the relationship between the party and government.

At some point, too much concern with the party would render him an ineffective and unfocused president. On the other hand, too much focus on government affairs would result in the party drifting away and the development of a vacuum at party leadership level – the same vacuum that created an opening for Zuma as a populist candidate. He is the first president of the country who had to fight for a second term as the president of the ANC in government, because the ANC was getting accustomed to replacing leadership whimsically. But Zuma also reflected how leadership has learned to manipulate the internal processes of the party and the institutions of the state to remain in power, irrespective of how party members feel. If indeed Zuma was to be the man of the people, with an unassailable connection to the broader masses outside and inside his party, he would not have had to make a case for his retention as the president of the ANC during the party's 2012 elective conference in Mangaung.

President Nelson Mandela did not have an interest in a second term either as party president or as president of the country. Had Mandela intended to continue for a second term, it would have been secured without a squabble within the ANC. President Thabo Mbeki also marched into his second term of the presidency without having to contest it. But Zuma had to make a case for the second term by getting internal party approval. His presidency came at a time when the ANC was constantly reviewing how it relates to government. This is not a stable environment, even though it is part of a working democracy. Jacob Zuma's presidency has not been the most stable. Internal party squabbles have intensified since his triumph at Polokwane in 2007. Perhaps all this has much to do with South Africa's political evolution, and Zuma's leadership just happens to find itself within these developments. Let us consider how South African politics appears to be developing, as Zuma is an interesting frame of reference to understand this.

Zuma's presidency is unfolding into an era that is identifiable and worthy of deep analysis. In some ways, justice has not been done to the man, because we are becoming a nation that perpetually seeks a scapegoat. Instead of confronting the evils of our society, we look for a way to normalise them, and thus ourselves, by pinning our failings on individuals. If Zuma is simply dubbed a 'failed leader', the nation will get to move on once he is gone, absolved and cleansed. In the eyes of some within the ANC, Mbeki was becoming a bad leader, and so the party, instead of looking inward, found in Mbeki a scapegoat for its own political shortcomings. So the ruling party unceremoniously removed him, and thereby cleansed itself of the sin it had committed by failing to transform into a modern political party.

As a society, it seems that we like to 'manufacture' leaders for our own convenience. And when things do not turn out the way we wanted them to, we simply demonise the leaders and blame them for all manner of uncomfortable socio-political developments. But usually the problem is much larger than one leader. In this case South Africa's downward trajectory cannot be blamed on Zuma alone. He is, after all, just one man and part of a much bigger system. Maybe the Zuma years will help South Africans realise that deeply ingrained problems are not solved by getting rid of one leader and replacing him with another. South Africa's problems are much bigger than Zuma. He has survived longer than most people thought possible, but one day he will go. And when he does, it certainly will not mean the end of our troubles.

TWO

——❦——

Zuma's bureaucratic empire

Two of the main reasons for Thabo Mbeki's downfall were that he was too bureaucratic, and too fond of concentrating power in his own hands. So the ANC got rid of Thabo and his old pipe. In came Jacob Zuma, a non-smoker and non-drinker, and many thought a new day had dawned. But now, oddly enough, and well into the second term of his presidency, Zuma presides over an even bigger empire of red tape – and the presidency has a much tighter stranglehold on effective governance.

After taking over as the president of the Republic of South Africa following the 2009 general elections, Jacob Zuma increased the size of the executive branch of government from 28 departments to 35,[1] with the National Planning Commission (NPC) being one of the most prominent additions to the public service. In his second term, which started in 2014, Zuma increased the number of departments to 37.[2] As a developing nation frustrated by poor delivery of public services, South Africans seem to tolerate any expansion of the public service, as long as it is presented as a

---

1 Xolani Mbanjwa, Justin Brown and Dewald van Rensburg, 'Time to down-size President Zuma', *City Press*, 21 February 2016. Available at city-press.news24.com. Accessed on 25 July 2016.
2 Alec Hogg, 'Full list of Jacob Zuma's administration – all the Ministers and Deputies', BizNews, 24 May 2014. Available at www.biznews.com. Accessed on 17 April 2015.

fix for poor performance. For this reason, the formation of the
NPC was welcomed without any critical evaluation.

The approach is quite simple. Identify a problem in the public
service and then create a department to deal with it specifically.
This is a self-justifying initiative showing that government does
care about resolving backlogs. What this approach lacks, however,
is the realisation that the problems did not arise because certain
institutions had not yet been invented to deal with them. No, the
problems appeared because the existing institutions could not
solve them. And that is why the creation of more institutions only
adds to the number of non-performing institutions. The best
alternative is to adjust existing departments to deal with the newly
identified problems. This type of response to problems is not
unique to South Africa. Big bureaucracies, often dysfunctional,
exist all over the world, even in advanced democracies such as the
United Kingdom.[3] It is a common practice for politicians, together
with their civil service counterparts, to grow government to an un-
recognisable behemoth capable of delivering nothing.

In an episode of my favourite TV series, *Yes Minister*, Jim Hacker,
the Minister of Administrative Affairs in the British government,
is confronted with the problem of big bureaucracy. Hacker's job is
to ensure that government departments deliver on their mandate,
and so he wants to cut government departments down to a more
manageable size. Mr Hacker's permanent secretary (in our system
the director-general), Humphrey Appleby, is only interested in ensuring that Hacker's department grows bigger and bigger. Why?
Because then the department can have the biggest budget! That

---

3   Philip Johnston, 'British bureaucracy is growing out of control', *The Tele-
    graph*, 18 January 2009. Available at www.telegraph.co.uk. Accessed on
    20 May 2015.

is all that matters to civil servants and their political masters: big departments with bigger budgets to play around with.

President Jacob Zuma's reordering of the public service confirms this approach. New departments and agencies were created to deal with identified failings, particularly poor planning in government. But there has been no attempt to identify those who were not doing their jobs in the government agencies that were there already. This approach simply gives the impression of being busy. Agencies focused on specific problems are mistaken for bodies with the ability to actually tackle those problems and resolve them.

By the end of Zuma's first term, in 2014, none of his newly created ministries and agencies – including his presidential hotline – had made any significant improvement in the public service. And this is despite the millions that have been spent on salaries and the operational costs of those newly created bodies.[4] In a sense, what Zuma has done is to create a 'big government' system that has not received any meaningful critical overview. That's because in South Africa, the existence of a problem-oriented government agency is accepted as an indication of focus and ability to resolve a problem. There is no discussion about big government.

Zuma appears more of a bureaucrat than Mbeki ever was. The establishment of the NPC, the Department of Planning, Monitoring and Evaluation and their clumsily articulated mandates seem to show that Zuma is also an Mbeki-style centralist! However, the departments he has established have yet to demonstrate their reasons for existence. A prime example is the Department of

---

4   Gareth van Onselen, 'R1.6 billion – what president Zuma's bloated Cabinet costs you', TimesLive, 23 November 2014. Available at www.timeslive.co.za. Accessed on 12 February 2016.

Economic Development, headed by Ebrahim Patel; it is not clear why this department was created.

But there's something even more crucial. An ever-growing government bureaucracy weighs on itself to such an extent that there is no clear chain of command. It's just not clear who's responsible for what. And Zuma the centralist located the NPC in the Office of the Presidency. I hold strong views on the commission – and how its operation impacts on bureaucratic efficiency in South Africa.

Despite being a democracy, the South African government occasionally shows a fascination for institutions that belong in dictatorial regimes. One such institution is the NPC, which was set up to 'develop a long-term development vision for government'. The main advantage touted for the commission was that it would provide much-needed long-term plans for South Africa. After all, it was often held that a lack of long-term planning had led to the electricity crisis, and to service delivery protests.

The NPC, it is stated, draws inputs from the wider public. Its notable character is that it promises to offer an opportunity to the public outside government to play a role and make suggestions to government planners. This is a noble call in the spirit of open democracy. But there is one thing we can't ignore: the commission was created out of frustration with a system in which government plans slowly trickle down through government departments. Policies and plans move from the ruling party manifesto down to Cabinet and then further down to ministries or government departments. This is consultative in the sense that plans pass through a process of filtering, refinement and adaptation. The plans pass through different departments as implementable yearly government programmes. By imposing the NPC as a body chaired and coordinated in the Presidency, the flow of responsibility and ultimately the line of accountability are watered down by the time a plan reaches the department that has to make it work.

The commission claims to have reached out to the people. It is tempting to argue that since it is open to the general public, it strikes a blow for democracy. But this depends heavily on whether the commission actually reflects the views of the public in the long-term plans it dreams up. Since the commission is chaired and coordinated in the Presidency, the final word on any plan may inevitably be that of the Presidency – and not of the people.

The idea that the commissioners represent society as a whole seems to be taken as an indication that planning is automatically democratic. This idea is misleading. Commissioners may merely provide a legitimising role and may sit on the commission only as symbols of the broader society. There is no proof that they take part in drawing up plans. The much-vaunted public approach of the commission is beginning to look like a way to legitimise choices made by the Presidency – and to disguise them as what the general public suggested. This type of outcome is actually a lot worse than the previous trickle-down process.

What I say here may seem obvious – that the idea of the NPC was flawed from the beginning. But the creation of the commission drew no criticism from well-informed observers and pundits. In most cases, when government announces an initiative, the pundits wait for it to be implemented before they give their views. While it may seem a logical and circumspect approach to wait before we pronounce on whether or not an initiative is sound, some projects need to be interrogated even before they are implemented.

But the establishment of the NPC was welcomed, with some lukewarm qualifications to the effect that success would depend on the calibre and character of the commissioners. The idea that they would be drawn from the general public, and would include independent academics and business people, seems to have convinced many commentators that the commission would be open and consultative. But no one raised the objection that superimposing a planning commission on top of existing government departments was never going to work. In my view, the commission is merely another boondoggle to create the impression that the president is doing something.

We don't need the commission because we already have the Medium Term Strategic Framework (MTSF), which relies on input from ministers, provincial premiers and directors-general. There is something fundamentally democratic and participatory about the manner in which each and every government department provides a realistic view of the challenges that confront it. A plan so derived cannot be said to be imposed from above. Challenges identified by individual departments and provincial governments are consolidated into a single strategic framework.

The horizontal positioning of government departments and agencies allows for an equitable contribution into government programmes. Even if we consider the reality that some departments, such as National Treasury, have more influence than others, the fact that all departments are represented means that it is a bottom-up process. This allows for a swift implementation of plans across government departments and agencies. The system allows for departments to group themselves to pursue outcomes. For example, the departments of Police, Justice and Correctional Services, Defence and Military Veterans, State Security, and Home Affairs work in a cluster called JCPS (Justice, Crime Prevention and Security) to improve safety and security as an outcome. But the so-called cluster system in South Africa is not pursued rigorously. National departments are not effectively held accountable on the basis of cluster outcomes. Instead, they account only on their specific departmental outputs. In a more rigorous application of a cluster system, government departments would account collectively by showing how their operations directly contribute to cluster outcomes. Using the JCPS cluster as an example, these departments would then collectively be held accountable on how exactly they have contributed to safety and security as a goal within the cluster. To fulfil this level of accountability, a mere statement by the department that their operations generally contribute to, say, safety and security would not suffice.

This system does not mean that departments deviate from the pursuit of their specific mandates. Instead, they account for individual mandates on one level, and on another level they must demonstrate how their individual operations contribute to broader government goals in the MTSF. This means departments and agencies could be tied to government goals instead of working in isolation. The cluster system could be tightened for a more rigorous pursuit of government targets.

The basic flaw in the NPC is that it sits on top of government departments and imposes a top-down power on government planning. National departments and agencies find it difficult to implement plans that are derived in this way. Apart from this awkward system, there is a lingering question: why should a full-fledged democracy adopt central planning? Central planning is essentially based on a siege mentality, and works better in non-democratic countries – usually in a war-economy situation. I suspect the existence of the commission frustrates national departments, which follow a wait-and-see scenario and no longer see fit to engage in bottom-up planning, but instead use the commission's top-down plans.

The adoption of the commission is an indication that Jacob Zuma is a bureaucrat whose manner of organising state administrative machinery is no different from that of Thabo Mbeki. In fact, Zuma seems to have accelerated the centralist process. For some, the growth of bureaucracy under Zuma is an indication of commitment to deliver services, and a boost for his image as a president who listens and responds to the people.

As part of Zuma's consolidation of bureaucracy, the Department of Minerals and Energy was split in two. The same thing happened with Education, as tertiary institutions were hived off into a Department of Higher Education and Training. And I must add the creation of the Ministry of Women, Children and People with Disabilities – run from the Presidency. In a sense, this type of reorganisation amounts to the proverbial shifting of chairs on the deck of the sinking ship.

But at least the president was seen to be doing something, and that in itself was an indication of commitment towards action, and ability to spur government into doing something. President Zuma's quest for a more visible government was also seen in the much-hyped creation of the presidential hotline, established in 2009. It was inaugurated under the directorship of a kwaito star, Eugene Mthethwa, and was meant to address the poor response of government departments, whose phones seemed to be permanently on voicemail.[5] The Planning, Monitoring and Evaluation department within the Presidency would also keep and evaluate a central depository of information about government progress.

But each and every government department already has monitoring and evaluation responsibilities. Individual departments may not have carried out these responsibilities due to lack of skills, capacity or the right attitude. It may be the case that for every

5   Mandy de Waal, 'Zuma hotline's puzzling statistics', *Mail & Guardian*, 27 January 2012. Available at mg.co.za. Accessed on 20 February 2016.

departmental oversight agency, there is an equivalent institution in the Presidency. With time, these parallel institutions may create confusion and undermine the development of government departments.

The Mbeki administration came under attack for its heavy bureaucracy, which was misdiagnosed and blamed on Mbeki's personal fascination with power. And now the Zuma administration is genuinely frustrated by the bureaucracy's inability to deliver on the party mandate, and also by its poor response to popular demands. But the two presidents are not that far apart in terms of how they organised the state bureaucracy. In fact, Zuma has in many ways intensified Mbeki's bureaucracy. Under Zuma, we have seen increased incorporation of institutions in the Presidency – the very problem that led to Mbeki's administration being characterised as too distant and disconnected from the ANC.

Zuma has failed to resolve the problem that partially carried him to power. He has failed to radically reverse the growth in the number of public servants. The growth in the public sector wage bill in effect 'crowds out all else',[6] reducing or undermining the government's ability to deliver even the bare minimum of services. The growth of the public sector is becoming a major concern. Once the state has entered into a phase of bureaucratisation, any leader who attempts to radically reverse it may be undermined by the global community. By this I mean finance and business, whose economic policy preferences are usually smoothly implemented under a rigid government bureaucracy. So, Zuma would appear delinquent if he tried to reverse or even halt the further growth of bureaucracy.

---

6   Linda Ensor, 'Public Sector wage bill crowds out all else', *Business Day*, 22 October 2015. Available at www.bdlive.co.za. Accessed on 2 August 2016.

Zuma has admitted that a democratic system is difficult to work through, and he would prefer 'dictatorship'. While campaigning ahead of the 2016 local government elections, he openly stated that:

> If you just give me six months to be a dictator, things will be straight . . . At the moment to take a decision, you need a resolution or petition. If it was up to me, education would be more than compulsory . . . if you are found walking in the streets, police would stop you and ask what is it that you're getting in the streets and not at school. If it was up to me, we would put stronger measures to ensure that in 30 years' time no one would be uneducated.[7]

This is not the first time that Zuma was unable to conceal his admiration for the type of decision-making process possible only under a dictatorship. In March 2015, he opened up about what he would do, if only he could be a dictator:

> If I was a dictator, I would change a few things . . . For an example I would say to a family, you need a house, here is the material and only bring the government person to supervise. Build your house. That is what I would say. And if they say they can't build, we will just get the person who can build; they must participate. If they can't put a brick they must mix the mud. So that there is a feeling that 'this is my own'.[8]

---

7 Karabo Ngoepe, 'Zuma: "If I was a dictator . . ."', News24, 22 July 2016. Available at www.news24.com. Accessed on 25 July 2016.
8 Qaanitah Hunter, 'Zuma: if I were a dictator . . .', Mail & Guardian, 25 March 2015. Available at mg.co.za. Accessed on 25 July 2015.

Zuma's impatience with democracy and the process of wider participation in decision-making could be inspired by the time he spends with his Chinese counterparts. Indeed democracy can be irritating, because it requires lengthy processes in terms of decision-making. But democracy also ensures that leaders account to the people. If it wasn't for democracy, Zuma might be able to deliver the goodies to this great nation of South Africa, but he might also help himself to state resources even more than he did with his Nkandla residence. While a first-year Politics student might argue that a dictatorship is a much better system than a democracy, it is unacceptable for the sitting president of a hard-won democracy to express such sentiments openly. This raises questions about what else the president would want to achieve with a short spell as a dictator. Given the grim legacy of apartheid, it is embarrassing for a South African president to yearn for dictatorship as a way of solving the country's problems.

The manner in which Zuma has arranged state bureaucracy, however, shows that he might be enjoying a bit of dictatorship in the manner in which his departments function and relate to each other. One need not be a dictator to undermine the democratic functioning of institutions. Even those who sit at the helm of democratic institutions can resort to desperate measures, measures that show their distaste for democracy as a way of addressing challenges in society. After all, US president Richard Nixon led a democratic state – and had taken an oath to serve and protect American democracy – but he abused democratic institutions to cover up the Watergate scandal, a massive abuse of power by a democratically elected leader.[9]

---

9   *The Washington Post*, 'Watergate', 14 June 2012. Available at www.washingtonpost.com. Accessed on 20 May 2016.

THREE

~~~

Capturing the state

The abrupt end of the apartheid system and the advent of democracy in 1994 posed many challenges for the incoming ANC as
custodians of the state and its people. The larger part of the history of the state in South Africa thus far had been that of a state
constituted to exclude the majority of the population. With the
collapse of apartheid, the ANC had to consider the question of
how the party ought to relate to the state, and the entities and
people within it. The ANC often maintains that during its fight
against apartheid, the party was simultaneously preparing to govern and thinking about the necessary institutional framework to
achieve this.[1] Quite often, the party refers to its 1992 policy document 'Ready to Govern'[2] as evidence that the party had reflected
on the challenges of governing even while engaged in the armed
struggle against the apartheid government. It is important to reflect
on whether the party's idea, that it has always been ready to govern, has been realistic, and what governing would entail as the
party sees it.

Governing involves a systematic way of relating to institutions
of authority, and of directing those institutions to achieve a set of

---

1   African National Congress (ANC), 'Strategy and Tactics', 1968. Available at
    www.marxists.org. Accessed on 25 July 2016.
2   African National Congress (ANC), 'Ready to Govern: ANC policy guideline
    for a democratic South Africa', 28–31 May 1992. Available at www.anc.org.za.
    Accessed on 25 July 2016.

goals. If a governing party fails to direct institutions to attain a set of agreed-upon goals, the institutions will take on a life of their own, and can be vulnerable to takeover by the powerful. The contest for state control would be one of the daunting tasks for the new ANC-led government. Here was a party with no experience of peaceful coexistence with the state, and then suddenly the party had to move the state in a desired direction. This exercise could have resulted in the ANC either being fully in control of the state, and therefore achieving its desired policy goals, or in the party constantly fighting to influence the direction of development within the state. That the ANC could capture the state did not necessarily mean that the party would direct that influence towards the public interest. The 'Ready to Govern' document does not see the possibility of the ANC itself being used to hijack the state towards the interests of the few. The document sees a benevolent ANC, acting mostly in the public interest. This suggests that the ANC sees the detractors to its policy objectives as coming from outside the party only, and not from insiders. Perhaps this explains why the party has not demonstrated any real plan to deal with internal problems.

During the Zuma presidency it has become clear that the 'enemies' of the ANC could well be nested within the party. Zuma has demonstrated that it is not only outsiders and right-wingers who are interested in capturing the state; it is at times ANC insiders, such as Zuma himself, who have become proxies to attempts by interest groups to capture the state. Yet, the news that the Gupta family has been running the state from the sidelines, through their influence on Zuma, has invoked only denials from the ANC. It is evident that the ANC's idea of state capture is framed in the context of colonisers and those aiming at regime change. This is a very narrow perspective.

The ANC has always had the suspicion that one of the challenges the party could face in the post-apartheid dispensation would be a business community that remains nostalgic about apartheid.[3] The idea that 'apartheid capital' was no longer comfortable with the continuation of the apartheid system did not convince the ANC that it would welcome ANC-led democratic governance. It was the ANC's perspective that apartheid capital only became concerned when apartheid policies began to pose limitations to access to the cheap labour required by the private sector. Historians such as Hermann Giliomee[4] have documented how the continuation of apartheid was becoming an inconvenience for the private sector. Further, international sanctions meant that South African companies could not trade freely outside the country. That the apartheid system denied the majority of the people an opportunity to earn a good livelihood by fully participating in the economy also implied that only a small section of the population could financially support local companies producing goods to be sold in South Africa.

There are those who argue that one of the reasons why the apartheid system collapsed was because the private sector was no longer willing to support the apartheid state. The ANC noted this point, but the party also realised that it would have to wrest control of the state from the private sector, to ensure that the party controlled the state in terms of the delivery of public goods, such as education, health, safety and security. From the ANC's point of view, the economy remains a crucial factor for the capture and control of the state. Therefore, influence on the private sector is

3 Amanda Khoza, 'Zuma bemoans racism, white capital', News24, 21 March 2016. Available at www.news24.com. Accessed on 10 May 2016.
4 Hermann Giliomee, 'Democratization in South Africa', in *Political Science Quarterly*, 110 (1), Spring 1995.

of critical importance for the ANC. Lack of influence on the private sector is a frustration that is littered all over the ANC's policy documents, with the party calling for 'the second phase of the transition'.[5] How, then, did the party seek to retain control of the state apparatus, including the economy? This is an interesting tale with remarkable twists that indicate the strength of the law of unintended consequences.

Convinced of the idea that the inherited apartheid private sector could not be trusted, the ANC sought to build an alternative private sector, otherwise referred to as the Black Economic Empowerment (BEE) project. This project started to take shape under Thabo Mbeki, whose administration sought to transform the economy, dominated by the white private sector, through the creation of new black capital that would fundamentally sympathise with the state's objectives. To the ANC, this new private sector would wrest control of the state from supposedly hostile forces, and would lodge control in the hands of the ANC. This was a straightforward transition, at least as far as the ANC was concerned. Needless to say, it did not work, for reasons the ANC could not have anticipated.

Transferring influence from the old private sector to a new, more sympathetic private sector was a key policy focus for Thabo Mbeki[6] and an essential element of the African Renaissance. From a moral point of view, there is an undeniable need for the transformation of the economy, to ensure that historically black, Indian and coloured South Africans get to play an active role. The original

5   African National Congress (ANC), 'The second transition: building a national democratic society and the balance of forces in 2012', 27 February 2012. Available at www.anc.org.za. Accessed on 25 July 2016.
6   Claire Tucker, 'Black economic empowerment and corporate governance', Bowman Gilfillan Africa Group, 7 October 2004. Available at www.bowman.co.za. Accessed on 20 June 2016.

thinking behind BEE might have been altruistic, but the manner in which it was pursued opened opportunities for those with sinister motives to loot the resources of the state under the guise of empowerment. In the end, as is often remarked,[7] ordinary people seem not to have gained much from the empowerment policy. But, most importantly, uncritical pursuit of black empowerment exposed the state to capture in a way that it is not yet completely acknowledged.

While the first group of beneficiaries of BEE emerged during the tenure of Nelson Mandela, a sizeable part of the black empowerment community came into being and thrived under Thabo Mbeki's regime. With some level of sophistication, and taking a jibe at the idea of continued domination of white capital in South Africa, Mbeki's project of creating a generation of BEE beneficiaries was well defended and did not spark outright public opposition. Mbeki was implementing ANC policy, a policy of normalising capital by ensuring that the black community is also reflected as a beneficiary. Today we can point to the likes of Patrice Motsepe and Cyril Ramaphosa as some of those who benefited from the first phase of the BEE project.

The idea of using government policy to create a sympathetic class of business has failed, and has left a legacy in which the capture of the state has become the motivator for accumulation by interest groups. When the ANC policies under Mbeki created a community of BEE beneficiaries awash with money and eager for further accumulation, it became clear that for this process of accumulation to be intensified, it was necessary that the state be under the control of ANC policy-makers who would then set new targets. The first generation of BEE beneficiaries showcased

---

7   *The Economist*, 'The president says it has failed', 31 March 2010. Available at www.economist.com. Accessed on 10 February 2016.

that it is possible to accumulate through capturing the state bureaucracy and then redistributing resources in line with desired
goals. The appetite for this pattern of accumulation, as generated
from the Mbeki era onwards, also brought with it the realisation
that state capture is a powerful political ideal.

'State capture' is a euphemism to describe a situation in which
the narratives, the direction and the value system of a society, including patterns of accumulation, are under the control of an elite
group. A World Bank discussion document defines it as '[t]he
efforts of a small number of firms (or such groups as the military,
ethnic groups and kleptocratic politicians) to shape the rules of
the game to their advantage through illicit, non-transparent provision of private gains to public officials'.[8]

The ANC's policy of BEE under Mbeki was carried out in a
way that sought to exert control on the state, its value system
and its grand narratives. One cannot just accumulate and push for
a project such as this without adopting the necessary narrative
through which such projects are justifiable and defensible in the
eyes of ordinary people. For the political elites to continue to have
a chance to wrest control of the state and its narratives, they also
need a strong entry narrative to open the way for their initiatives.
Transformation is a legitimate objective, and transformation of the
private sector into black hands is a more specific way of going
about this. The rhetoric of transformation was amplified by ANC
policy thinking under Mbeki. Transformation is a genuine objective for a democratic South Africa. After all, it is essential that
the end of apartheid actually meant the end of domination by a
small section of the population in the economy and other areas
of life. In practice, however, for the ANC 'transformation' means

---

8   The World Bank, 'State capture', discussion paper, 21 May 2001. Available
    at www.worldbank1.org. Accessed on 20 May 2016.

capturing the state by creating a sympathetic business elite who will assist the party to further influence the direction, values and also the narratives within the state. A reading of Marxist theory[9] shows that business elites within the state often behave in the same way, even if they were created for a different purpose.

For example, by creating new black elites through state apparatus, the ANC ended up with the classic problem of a class of business people whose creation does not benefit ordinary people or the country as a whole. Even worse, the creation of the BEE class increased the appetite of interest groups to capture the state for their own interests, and not to further the ANC's transformation imperatives.

When Thabo Mbeki's administration came to an end, a new group of elites came to dominate the ANC, and just like those before them they wanted a turn at the feeding trough. As their predecessors showed, the state is important in order to sustain a pattern of accumulation that seems to benefit only a few.

By the time Zuma took over as president of the ANC, perceptions of BEE were changing. The suspicion was setting in that BEE might not improve ordinary people's lives. Many South Africans were waking up to the dim reality that politicians often do not deliver on promises. While Thabo Mbeki rode the wave of Mandela euphoria,[10] and used it to his advantage, Zuma had to deal with an angry and disillusioned nation.

Thabo Mbeki presided over state capture; however, his style of engaging with the public did not push the ANC onto the defensive about who was attempting to capture the state and for what

---

9   Peter Bell and Harry Cleaver, 'Marx's theory of crisis as a theory of class struggle', *The Commoner,* Autumn 2002.

10 *The Baltimore Sun,* 'Rainbow realities South Africa: As euphoria over Mandela leadership wanes, disillusionment setting in', 18 August 1997. Available at articles.baltimoresun.com. Accessed on 20 July 2016.

purpose. Mbeki himself would probably have pointed out that the state was already subject to capture from foreign and white capital. Thus, Mbeki would defend his project not as state capture but as the freeing of the state from the control of interest groups. Zuma has tried this explanation, but it has not worked for reasons that have to do with his personal lack of credibility and not-so-convincing skills as an interlocutor. His shot at state capture has merely ushered in a less sophisticated and more abrasive episode of a phenomenon that was underway long before he took over as president. Mbeki the centrist did such a crafty job at this that there was not even a public debate about state capture. Instead, the issue was that he centralised power in his office and was not consultative.

Under Zuma's leadership, however, it has become clear that the state is being captured to further the interests of his family and his friends, including the Gupta family. The ANC, at least under Mbeki's leadership, and also perhaps while the party was preparing to govern, probably did not foresee the possibility that its attempts to retain control of important parts of the state in order to achieve its policy goals would be an initiative that could be interrupted by other forces. The Zuma years, particularly the manner in which Zuma has related to the state bureaucracy, have highlighted the reality that the ANC could be used to capture the state in the interests of a few connected individuals, such as the Gupta family. Previously, the idea of state capture was seen as something that could only be perpetrated by Western businesses acting in the interests of foreign powers, such as the United States and Great Britain. This idea has preoccupied the ANC and its alliance part-ners (e.g., the SACP)[11] to a point where it has blinded them to the reality that the ANC itself can be subject to state capture.

---

11 Fose Segodi, 'SACP threatens mass action against state capture', *Mail & Guardian*, 6 June 2016. Available at mg.co.za. Accessed on 20 July 2016.

The ANC's suspicion about the role of the private sector in post-apartheid South Africa is genuine. Also genuine is the party's naivety about the real threat of state capture from within the party itself. The party will have to wake up to the idea that its own members are potential proxies for state capture, as demonstrated by Zuma's relationship with the Gupta family.

Having had to confront the reality that there are indeed attempts at state capture, and that the perpetrators are not the usual suspects backed by Western powers, the ANC has resigned itself to the standard explanation that the party is under siege by corporations with the aim of undermining Zuma's administration in particular, and the ANC government in general. This is how the party managed to find its way out of Zuma's blunder in replacing Finance minister Nhlanhla Nene with the 'little-known'[12] Des van Rooyen, in December 2015. The decision sent the markets into free fall, with the rand crashing.[13] Realising that his decision was disastrous, Zuma capitulated and a few days later appointed former Finance minister Pravin Gordhan* to replace Van Rooyen. Then the spin began as to how to clean up the fallout from a decision that was quantified as having cost financial markets an estimated R500 billion.[14]

* At the time of going to print Gordhan was still Minister of Finance, but there was speculation that he might be charged by the Hawks and forced to resign.

12 Matuma Letsoalo, 'Nhlanhla Nene removed as finance minister', *Mail & Guardian*, 9 December 2015. Available at mg.co.za. Accessed on 1 March 2016.
13 Sam Mkokeli, Carol Paton, Phakamiza Ndzamela and Linda Ensor, 'Rand crash after Zuma fires Nene', *Business Day*, 10 December 2015. Available at www.bdlive.co.za. Accessed on 10 April 2016.
14 Alec Hogg, 'Zuma on Nenegate: "markets overreacted to the firing." Rand tanks again', BizNews, 11 January 2016. Available at www.biznews.com. Accessed on 25 January 2016.

Questions were immediately raised about what could have been Zuma's reasons for taking such a drastic – and clearly disastrous – decision. It emerged subsequently that the Gupta family had earlier 'offered' Nene's job to deputy Finance minister Mcebisi Jonas.[15] Jonas confirmed in a statement, which he read on live television, that the Gupta family had indeed approached him, and offered him the job of heading the National Treasury. With allegations mounting that the Guptas had been deploying ministers to key government positions, the media started zooming in on the issue of state capture. The ANC switched into public relations mode, with the party's secretary-general, Gwede Mantashe, angrily making public remarks about the danger of state capture and its negative implications for democracy.[16]

It is very interesting how the Gupta saga reformulated the state capture debate. Some people[17] were bold enough to say that there has been state capture since the end of apartheid, and that the main concern with the Guptas is that they do not represent the traditional face of capital, meaning they are neither white nor Western. The concept of state capture then became more abstract. As the debate raged, Zuma gained a reprieve regarding the extent to which the Gupta family have him in their pockets. The ANC initiated an inquiry into state capture, and asked those with evidence to submit it to Gwede Mantashe's office. In my opinion, it is impossible for the ANC to investigate a case in which the party is itself the main player.

15 Thanduxolo Jika, Qaanitah Hunter and Sabelo Skiti, 'How Guptas shopped for new minister', *Sunday Times*, 13 March 2016. Available at www.timeslive.co.za. Accessed on 10 May 2016.

16 Sam Mkokeli, 'Mantashe outflanked on state capture fight', *Business Day*, 1 June 2016. Available at ww.bdfm.co.za. Accessed on 10 April 2016.

17 Andile Mngxitama, 'Guptas are just red herring', Independent Online, 16 February 2016. Available at www.iol.co.za. Accessed on 20 May 2016.

If the ANC was serious about investigating alleged state capture, the party would have opted for an inquiry to take place outside the party. In order to capture the state, it requires that the party be influenced. It is pointless to expect the party to investigate how it has been influenced, particularly if the influence seems to come through the party leader. Even more challenging is the reality that the state does not belong to the ANC, so it cannot be the ANC that investigates state capture. Only credible institutions within the state itself can carry out such an investigation. But from the start it was clear that the ANC wanted to do the investigation itself in order to control the outcome.

It was therefore no surprise when the ANC secretary-general announced that the investigation into state capture had not yielded any results;[18] effectively, state capture was not underway, at least not as far as Zuma and the Gupta family are concerned. The SACP was not happy with the results of the inquiry; the party stated that there is a clear case of influence on government by the Gupta family. The leader of the Young Communist League said that under Zuma corruption has been 'institutionalised and legalised'.[19]

The closing of the ANC's inquiry into state capture did not lay to rest the question at hand. The question is, why is the control of the National Treasury so important for the project of Zuma and his allies? It is also necessary to confront the reality of competing interests at the centre of state capture. First, the ANC seems to believe that the party ought to control the state, and that this can be achieved by creating an alternative capitalist class – progressive

18 Ranjeni Munusamy, 'Gupta Continua: Guptas triumph as the ANC shuts down state capture probe', Daily Maverick, 1 June 2016. Available at www.dailymaverick.co.za. Accessed on 10 July 2016.
19 Sihle Manda, 'Young Reds lash out', Independent Online, 6 June 2016. Available at www.iol.co.za. Accessed on 5 July 2016.

capital. If this is still the ANC's belief, it is important to probe the ongoing attempts to bring the Treasury into line. Whose interests are actually served by control of the National Treasury?

Thabo Mbeki shielded the National Treasury from direct political threats or interest groups. An indication of this can be seen in the way Mbeki repelled Cosatu's and the SACP's populist criticism of the Treasury for pursuing fiscal discipline. Mbeki's pursuit of the Growth, Employment and Redistribution (Gear) macro-economic policy required that the Treasury be shielded from public assault by the left-leaning labour movement.[20] This is also because the Treasury was not hostile to any of his projects, including Gear. Even more beneficial to Mbeki was that, during his tenure as president, the general public had lower expectations of accountability, which meant less disruption when it came to implementation of public policy. The idea that a leader and his cabal could squander public resources was not understood as a reality at that time. This was in the wake of the glorious Mandela years, and the government and the political elites were still basking in Mandela's glory. Under such circumstances, the Treasury was not at a point where it saw the need to aggressively protect public resources from the very political elites responsible for governing.

Under Zuma the picture changed dramatically, and there arose a heightened sense of the need to protect public resources against the dominant political elites. Zuma's administration ushered in a deep suspicion about the motives of the political elites. This is not to say that Zuma was the first leader to do wrong things. It did mean, however, that his ascension coincided with rising suspicion of political elites. Perhaps this suspicion would have emerged with

---

20 John Haylett, 'South Africa: ANC leaders attack Cosatu', *International Journal of Socialist Renewal*, 5 November 2010.

or without Zuma. Perhaps Zuma was merely unlucky in the sense that his administration coincided with the end of the Mandela glory days. This could also mean that Mbeki's administration, its policy implementation and worldviews about politics, including race relations, accelerated the end of the glory days, and created the space for the emergence of a brand of politics dominated by suspicion and lack of trust of politicians.

What can be said with certainty is that Zuma's conduct in government has justified the public suspicion of politicians, and has consequently raised people's demand for accountability on the part of government. If that is the case, and I believe it is, Zuma's administration – particularly his aggressive distaste for accountability – naturally drove institutions such as the National Treasury to define themselves against the looting of state resources by Zuma's cronies. Under Zuma's administration, the brazen nature of corruption and the violation of rules of accountability have resulted in a situation where state institutions have to take a stand either against or in support of his project. Under Mbeki, the battle was not as openly declared, and Mbeki's diplomatic nature and evasive stance on issues allowed for institutions to remain relatively neutral towards his project, while effectively not opposing his plans. Under Mbeki, the National Treasury could afford to stay out of the 'politics of the belly', because it and other state institutions were not expected to take a position in relation to the president's plans.

The recent debacle over the control of the National Treasury indicates that the situation regarding state capture has become brazen and transparent, such that many institutions of state have been forced to pick a side. The courts have taken a strong stance by stating unequivocally that corruption is a real scourge, and the

Public Protector's office deserves praise in this respect.[21] On the one hand, the prosecution authorities and the police – the crime prevention cluster – have taken a position in support of Zuma, and investigations into matters that could implicate Zuma have been thwarted. On the other hand, the National Treasury has taken a position against Zuma[22] by raising the alarm about the high level of corruption, and by questioning proposed expenditure that is blatantly in the interests of the few (read: Zuma's allies).

This is the reason why Zuma sees it as important to bring the Treasury back under his control. Zuma inherited Mbeki's Treasury, and he is working hard to convert it. This has pushed the Treasury to take a position, with Finance minister Pravin Gordhan accelerating his crusade against Zuma and corruption in general. Zuma's attempt to rein in the Treasury in December 2015 by appointing his ally failed, and he was forced to make a U-turn by bringing back Gordhan, who seems to enjoy a good relationship with the markets. It is naive to think that Zuma would give up in his attempt to install a different minister at the Treasury. The president is aware that perseverance is required to complete his project of capturing key government institutions, such as the Treasury. Gordhan's position as Finance minister is untenable, given that the minister is openly at war with the president. Ministers serve at the pleasure of the president. It seems that Zuma feels the markets hold him ransom when it comes to exercising his executive privilege to decide who serves in his Cabinet;

21 Naledi Shange, 'Quotes from Chief Justice Mogoeng Mogoeng's Nkandla judgment', News24, 31 March 2016. Available at www.news24.com. Accessed on 20 July 2016.

22 Stephen Grootes and Rahima Essop, 'Battle lines drawn in Gordhan vs Zuma war', Eyewitness News, 29 February 2016. Available at ewn.co.za. Accessed on 20 June 2016.

Gordhan is a market minister, and Zuma wants his own man in that position.

Realising that his return to the Finance portfolio has propelled him to stardom, Gordhan has used his position to his advantage. Unlike Zuma, Gordhan has the markets in his corner, and he is also an expert in using the media to build the image of someone who is protecting state resources against the depredations of Zuma and his allies, including the Gupta family. Zuma's strategy is clearly to isolate Gordhan, by giving him a long rope to hang himself with. By resorting to press conferences and speaking of himself as an 'activist', Gordhan has broken the code of allegiance to the ANC. His enemies in the ANC can use this to accuse him of airing the party's dirty laundry in public, and of being captured by corporate interests.

It is untenable for Gordhan to continue in his position when he is openly defiant towards Zuma's project. He has raised concerns about the decision to proceed with the nuclear deal with the Russians, openly stating that the deal is too expensive and may not be in the best interests of South Africa.[23] He has also sought to deal with rampant maladministration within state-owned entities such as South African Airways.[24] Further, he is a nuisance to local government tsars, who are often corrupt and who fail to deliver services for communities. This is too big a mandate to be shouldered by a single department within the executive. Ministers are generally prone to spend more in their departments, and increasing their budgets is a sign of importance. Wastage is part

23 Jan-Jan Joubert, 'Treasury puts brakes on nuclear spend', TimesLive, 24 February 2016. Available at www.timeslive.co.za. Accessed on 10 March 2016.
24 Emily Corke, 'Gordhan endorses Nene's decision on SAA/Airbus deal', Eyewitness News, 22 December 2015. Available at ewn.co.za. Accessed on 20 July 2015.

of the commotion. Therefore, one way or another, Pravin Gordhan's Treasury will have to keep on saying 'no' to other government departments, since the minister's return to Treasury is solely justified by his ability to say 'no' to maladministration. If Gordhan lives up to expectations from the general public and accountability activists by continuing to say 'no' to government departments who waste money, he will eventually find himself isolated even from the moderates within government. This could mean that he will find it difficult to secure backers in government, and it could make his position as Minister of Finance untenable. Zuma has been fighting Gordhan indirectly through the investigation of the minister's role in the so-called rogue unit within the South African Revenue Service (SARS),[25] which allegedly illegally gathered intelligence on targeted individuals. Even if Zuma's tactic does not work, it is quite possible that Gordhan will eventually tire of the battle against Zuma and resign. The ANC tradition is such that mavericks are not to be tolerated, even if they take a principled stance. The collective wins, one way or another.

The main reason why Gordhan continues to hold as one of the remaining obstacles to state capture is because Zuma does not want to upset the markets in the way he did when he fired Nhlanhla Nene. The concern within the ANC, despite divisions that may exist within the party, is that it is too risky to engage in fights on too many fronts at the same time. The party is struggling to convince ordinary South Africans that, despite the noise made by the opposition, the ANC has a legitimate right to make decisions and govern. The party is concerned with the reality of

---

25 Marianne Thamm, 'SARS rogue unit controversy', Daily Maverick, 3 December 2015. Available at www.dailymaverick.co.za. Accessed on 10 April 2016.

unemployment, and it has to convince the masses of unemployed youth that it has a solution. There are also the many scandals around Zuma himself, which raise concerns about the credibility of the leadership the ANC provides. All of this dictates that a direct confrontation with the markets is political suicide. Hence the party might wait and fight one battle at a time. In the meantime, the ANC has resorted to the classic explanation that the Treasury is a stumbling block to transformation. It has allegedly been captured by interest groups, the so-called Stellenbosch mafia, who want to maintain their grip on the state through control of key institutions, such as the Treasury. This is flipping the script, but Zuma's hold on the ANC will ensure that this script gains resonance within the party.

Through his capture of the ANC, Zuma has a good opportunity to reformulate the debate on state capture, and to ensure that the ANC appears to be a victim in an environment dominated by foreign capital and local collaborators. The party's compliant auxiliary bodies – the ANC Women's League, ANC Youth League and Umkhonto we Sizwe Military Veterans' Association – do not need to be convinced of this idea; they are already propagating it. In his route towards ensuring the capture of the state, Zuma first had to capture the ANC, a task he accomplished well.

In order to capture the state, it is necessary to bring key institutions into alignment. Capturing a political party ensures that there is no political recourse against those who seek to capture the state. Capture of the criminal justice system ensures there are no meaningful investigations into corruption and the diversion of state resources. This is a complex project that involves different battles along the way. Zuma's efforts in this regard began with the capture of the ANC, a necessary step on the road to state capture.

FOUR

Zuma vs the judiciary

President Jacob Zuma is the only president in post-apartheid South Africa who has had both institutional and personal quarrels with the justice system. The president's own quarrels with the judiciary have had a deep impact on how people see his relationship with the institutions that deliver justice. Some of these quarrels were already heating up when Zuma took over from Thabo Mbeki. The decision to dissolve the elite criminal investigation unit, the Scorpions,[1] was made under Mbeki's administration and was subsequently challenged by activists during Zuma's tenure as president. The court's ruling on this matter was delivered in 2011.[2]

Then there was a court challenge started by the arms deal critics Terry Crawford-Browne and Richard Young, requesting the Constitutional Court to order an inquiry into 'defence procurement', otherwise referred to as the 'arms deal'. The decision to procure arms to re-equip the South African National Defence Force (SANDF) was taken and executed in 1999, during Mbeki's term of office.[3] The court's decision on the call for instituting an inquiry

---

1   Wendell Roelf, 'Parliament: Scorpions will be dissolved', *Mail & Guardian*, 30 June 2008. Available at mg.co.za. Accessed on 20 February 2016.
2   Ernest Mabuza and Sam Mkokeli, 'Damning Scorpions judgment damaging to ANC', *Business Day*, 18 March 2011. Available at www.bdlive.co.za. Accessed on 10 March 2015.
3   *City Press*, 'Mbeki, Manuel to give evidence at arms deal commission', News24, 16 June 2013. Available at www.news24.com. Accessed on 27 July 2016.

into the arms deal, following Crawford-Browne's relentless pursuit of the matter, was on course to be delivered under Zuma's administration. About five months before the Constitutional Court was due to rule on an open inquiry, Zuma jumped the gun by setting up a commission of inquiry under Judge Willie Seriti.[4]

If the Mbeki administration had fully addressed the controversial arms deal by allowing a much wider investigation, instead of the limited one that took place, Zuma would not have had to deal with the problem, and would not have had to act to avoid a damaging Constitutional Court decision on the matter. The court would have most certainly ruled in favour of Crawford-Browne. By acting on the matter before the court could decide upon it, Zuma avoided a judgment that could have questioned the legality of the arms deal, and instead ordered an inquiry with probing and stringent terms. By moving proactively, Zuma gained the leverage to manage the scope of the inquiry because he set the terms of reference.

An additional inherited problem for Zuma related to the appointment of the National Director of Public Prosecutions (NDPP), the head of the National Prosecuting Authority (NPA). Former president Thabo Mbeki had suspended the then NDPP, Vusi Pikoli, in September 2007 due to the alleged 'breakdown of trust' between Pikoli and the then Justice minister, Brigitte Mabandla, over Pikoli's pursuit of national police commissioner Jackie Selebi on corruption charges.[5] When Zuma became president, he had to appoint a new NDPP, and he chose Advocate Menzi Simelane, the

---

4   Fin24, 'Judges named for arms deal probe', 24 October 2011. Available at
    www.fin24.com. Accessed on 20 June 2015.
5   Franny Rabkin, 'Mbeki says he suspended Pikoli because he risked national
    security', *Business Day*, 8 February 2016. Available at www.bdlive.co.za.
    Accessed on 29 July 2016.

former director-general in the Department of Justice. The decision to appoint Simelane proved to be a wrong turn.

One would have expected Zuma to stay clear of the already-
compromised Simelane when he came to power. Simelane's appointment was challenged on the basis of views he had expressed
during Mbeki's term, views that showed a lack of respect for the
principle that the NPA needed to be independent from the executive in exercising its duties. The appointment of Simelane
became a nightmare for the presidency. First, the opposition
Democratic Alliance (DA) complained that Zuma's choice of
Simelane to lead the NPA was irrational. The only logical reason
for the appointment was Simelane's staunch support for Zuma.
In Simelane's testimony before the Ginwala Commission of
Inquiry, which was set up to examine Pikoli's fitness to hold
office, it emerged that he did not see any problem with the prosecutor being directed by the executive (the Department of Justice)
when it came to decisions to prosecute. In his tenure as director-
general, Simelane had written a letter that showed interference
with a decision by the NDPP to prosecute.[7] In ruling on Simelane's
fitness to hold office as NDPP, the Constitutional Court would
rely on his conduct and on his testimony before the Ginwala commission, raising serious concerns about his respect for the rule of
law and the Constitution. Simelane became Zuma's most controversial appointment when the court ruled that Zuma was not
thinking rationally in appointing Simelane.[8]

Zuma has had a great opportunity to shape the judiciary, a

6   News24, 'Zuma defends Simelane appointment', 20 May 2010. Available
    at www.news24.com. Accessed on 29 July 2016.
7   Sello S Alcock, 'How Justice DG will be probed', *Mail & Guardian*, 27
    March 2009. Available at mg.co.za. Accessed on 20 June 2016.
8   Niren Tolsi, 'ConCourt confirms Menzi Simelane's appointment invalid', *Mail
    & Guardian*, 5 October 2012. Available at mg.co.za. Accessed 10 August 2016.

chance that some presidents never get. Zuma was fortunate to be able to appoint the chief justice of the Constitutional Court, the highest court in the land. And he appointed a young chief justice, someone who could shape the course of the Constitutional Court for many years to come. Zuma has clearly demonstrated that he wants to transform the judiciary – whichever way he can. The suspicion is that he is motivated by his brushes with the law, both as a leader and as an individual. South Africa, despite its rotting political machinery, has one of the most robust and independent judiciaries in the world. However, international adulation has not been enough to protect our judiciary from attack at home. That said, there is a need for South Africa to engage in a deeper reflection on the role of the judiciary – in a society that desperately needs transformation.

Thabo Mbeki did not attempt to engage openly with the judiciary. He was fully conversant with the nuances and wanted to be seen as someone who fully respects judicial independence. Zuma's approach is different. He has been more open about his discomfort. Under Zuma's administration, the conflict between the judiciary and the executive has been more in the open[9] and has not been expressed in evasive terms.

An open debate about court judgments and the role of the judiciary in itself is not a bad thing at all. On the contrary, in a healthy democracy, tension between the executive and the judiciary is completely normal. Zuma's tendency to raise issues with the work of the judiciary is therefore permissible. The problem, however, is his numerous personal brushes with the judiciary, which include his rape trial, accusations of corruption and the excessive public expenditure on his private home at Nkandla. Needless to say, the

9   Moshoeshoe Monare, 'ANC contempt for judiciary cause for alarm', *Mail & Guardian*, 26 June 2015. Available at mg.co.za. Accessed on 27 July 2016.

president's record compromises the legitimacy of his attempts to engage the country in a meaningful conversation about the role of the judiciary. The many court challenges against Zuma, and the many questionable decisions made by his administration, also make him a liability in any debate on the transformation of the judiciary. This debate may be sound and necessary, but because of his track record one cannot dismiss the possibility that the president has a personal vendetta against the judiciary as an institution.

At a time when Zuma once again faces the possibility of being prosecuted for corruption, it is understandable that people are sceptical whenever he questions or criticises the judiciary. The Supreme Court of Appeal ruled in 2016 that the NPA's decision in 2009 to cease prosecution against Jacob Gedleyihlekisa Zuma was reviewable by the court.[10] The DA had embarked on the process of accessing the 'spy tapes' – clandestine recordings of conversations in 2007 between then NPA head Bulelani Ngcuka and Scorpions boss Leonard McCarthy over when to charge Zuma – as necessary material for the court to undertake a review of the NPA's decision in April 2009 to drop the charges against Zuma. The DA has successfully kept alive the possibility that the NPA's decision to drop the 700-odd corruption charges can be reversed. This simply says that Jacob Zuma could still face prosecution on charges relating to the corruption conviction of his one-time financial advisor, Schabir Shaik. The case is to be finalised by the Constitutional Court, whose decision could see Zuma once more facing corruption charges.[11]

10 Phillip de Wet, 'Timeline: How the spy tapes saga continues to haunt Zuma since 2001', *Mail & Guardian*, 23 May 2016. Available at mg.co.za. Accessed on 20 June 2016.
11 Franny Rabkin, 'NPA turns to top court to appeal ruling on spy tapes', *Business Day*, 8 July 2016. Available at www.bdlive.co.za. Accessed on 27 July 2016.

President Zuma is clearly having a protracted conflict with the judiciary, the result of which is a missed opportunity to engage on the subject of transformation of the judiciary. He is compromised when it comes to driving a meaningful discussion and contribution on shaping the direction of the judiciary. For example, his decision to appoint Judge Mogoeng Mogoeng as chief justice was met with criticism from the media and civil society. The manner in which Mogoeng's nomination and confirmation by the president was handled in the public arena shows that the president has lost authority when it comes to dealing with the judiciary.

But if you take a step back and try to see his judicial philosophy, Mogoeng was not a bad candidate at all. His judgment on Nkandla – that Zuma has to pay back some of the money spent on his private home – has earned Justice Mogoeng the utmost respect as a defender of the Constitution. What seems to have been the problem is this: Mogoeng was appointed by President Jacob Zuma, who is perceived as someone who can't be trusted to get anything right when it comes to the judiciary, or with the police and justice cluster. So Mogoeng was simply ridiculed without any deep reflection on his qualities.

Rubbished as a hot Protestant homophobic fanatic, Mogoeng was met with insults and dismissal by the media following the news of his nomination to serve as chief justice. Some people dismissed him as inexperienced, and thought he was simply the president's church buddy. His appointment was seen as an act of lunacy by the president, an attempt to reward the faith community. Some feared Moegoeng would reverse certain civil liberties that have been won over the years, particularly the rights of gays. During his interview by the Judicial Service Commission (JSC), his statements that God wants him to be the chief justice seemed to affirm an obsession with the biblical route as opposed to the constitutional route.

But media commentators judged Mogoeng too quickly and un-fairly. More often than not, South Africans shy away from discussing religion as an influence on their political outlook. Whenever religion, particularly Christianity, becomes part of the discourse, powerful commentators tend to dismiss the religious angle. This drives the perception that there is only a stark choice between a democracy and a theocracy. But many South African voters seem to find comfort in the idea that the chief justice is a staunch Christian.

Mogoeng's nomination could have been seen in the context of appeasing the Christian constituency in South Africa, which is a larger proportion of the population than is the non-Christian. In the past few years some progressive legislation did raise concerns within the Christian community. Among such laws is the Civil Union Act, which sought to recognise same-sex marriage. Some communities saw it as an abomination. Most importantly, parliament did not proactively engage in the process of drafting and passing the law. It was passed after the Constitutional Court found the existing Marriage Act inadequate – because it violated the right not to be discriminated against on the basis of sexual orientation. The law was passed reluctantly as a constitutional obligation, rather than out of devotion towards civil liberties.

Parliament was therefore compelled by the court to pass a law to correct a situation in which same-sex marriage was not recognised. The Civil Union Act was then passed to provide recognition of same-sex marriage and thus ensure compliance with the Constitution, but the new law did not enjoy popular support among Christians. However, it is not a requirement that all laws need to satisfy the majority of the population. And those laws must comply with the Constitution because South Africa is a constitutional democracy – where the Constitution is the highest law in the land.

But where citizens are concerned about what they consider to be the moral implications of a law, they have a right to raise such concerns. If their objection is based on their religious beliefs, this should be stated and discussed openly. The Constitution was not dropped from heaven; it was made by the people and it can be amended by the people.

On that basis, the appointment of a Chief Justice who is seen as a Christian fundamentalist should not be regarded as an aberration. The existence of concerns about the constitutional acknowledgement of same-sex marriage means that there is a space in South Africa for a judge who is openly opposed to it.

Then there is the law that legalised abortion. This upset some Christians, who are against what they call 'killing of unborn babies'. The power dynamics among South Africans on issues of this nature may create the impression that everyone is happy and content with such legislation. The domination of this perception in the public arena – particularly in formal civil society circles – is responsible for the way in which appointments such as that of Mogoeng are ridiculed and mishandled. And it is difficult to cast a wider perspective on the appointment of a Christian judge such as Mogoeng, since Zuma is seen as a nuisance to the justice system. The nomination and appointment of Mogoeng has not sparked the debate and searching inquiry it deserves. This is for two reasons: the first is disregard for the Christian position in a secular democracy, and the second is the baggage Jacob Zuma brings to the judiciary.

While attention has been focused on his personal and official squabbles with the law, Zuma has been forthright in his intention to shape the future of the judiciary. But some commentators think Zuma does not possess an unbiased agenda for transforming the judiciary. He is seen as a man with a simple mission – to survive his personal battles with the law. He seems determined to push ahead with the transformation of the judiciary in his own way. And if he does so, this could cast him as the president who had the guts to challenge the untouchable judiciary. In that case, any judgment against him by the courts could be seen as a vendetta by judges against a man who dared to talk straight to them. The Zuma presidency has already cast itself as an administration under siege from the courts.

That said, the president will leave behind a lasting legacy with his appointment of Chief Justice Mogoeng. In Mogoeng we have a proud and openly conservative judge, with a distinct judicial philosophy. He may have a narrowly formulated understanding of the role of the Constitution, but this aspect was not brought up during his confirmation and interview before the JSC. Instead he was ridiculed as an evangelical fanatic.

Zuma marched ahead with Mogoeng's appointment to lead the Constitutional Court, effectively a vote of no confidence in the deputy chief justice, Dikgang Moseneke, widely seen as the natural successor to the position of chief justice. Legal circles and civil society organisations saw Moseneke as an experienced judge who understood how the court ought to relate to the executive.

It is said that Moseneke's private utterances at his 60th birthday party in 2008, when he reportedly expressed his commitment to uphold what is right for the people as opposed to what is right for the ANC, may have cost him the position of chief justice. But this seems too trivial a reason for a president to overlook someone fit for a high and influential position. Perhaps the main reason why Zuma was not comfortable with Moseneke is simply because he represents a judicial philosophy that Zuma does not believe in. In most of his well-crafted judgments, Moseneke comes across as a radical, and this can be traced back to his Pan Africanist Con-

gress (PAC) roots. Hardly a judge who holds back, Moseneke believes the Constitutional Court should interpret the Constitution
to acknowledge the need for radical transformation of our society.

For Moseneke, the state has a responsibility to implement policies such as affirmative action to address past apartheid injustices
inflicted by the state. He is a defender of state intervention, a progressive and a judicial constructivist. Moseneke's judgments are
generous and expressive. He believes in state intervention while at
the same time being vociferous when it comes to the executive's
indulgence. He came out very strongly against Zuma's decision to
extend the tenure of Chief Justice Sandile Ngcobo, saying it was
not only against the law, but also outright offensive. So why was
Moseneke not appointed to head the Constitutional Court?

Not all presidents get an opportunity to appoint the chief justice of the highest court in the land. At first it seemed like Zuma
had scored big, but then Mogoeng showed he is not just a Zuma
puppet. It has been on his watch that the Constitutional Court
found that Zuma had breached the Constitution in his response
to the Public Protector's report on Nkandla. Mogoeng also turned
out to be not as biblically inclined as observers had feared, perhaps to Zuma's disappointment.

But Zuma's conversation with the judiciary is not limited to
the appointment of judges. Zuma has no problem whatsoever in
turning the heat on the judiciary over the impact of their rulings
on transformation, particularly when rulings by the judiciary cross
paths with the ANC's transformation agenda. This is a reflection
of how the ANC as a political party has chosen to relate to power,
while at the same time occupying power.

It was very interesting to see the Zuma government issue a discussion paper purporting to 'assess the judgments that have been
made by the judiciary', with the focus on seeing how this impacts

upon transformation and the functioning of government.[12] This is a nicely worded initiative that, at first glance, is aimed merely at understanding the decisions made by the judges. Released by the Justice department in March 2012, the discussion document shows a government willing to study the decisions of the courts in order to effect changes and improvement in the way government executes policy. But a closer observation – and taking the context into consideration – indicates that government actually wants to review these court decisions. The way the government keeps on appealing decisions by the judiciary shows that it has no confidence in the judiciary. An example can be seen in the government's appeal of the decision by the High Court in April 2016 that corruption charges against President Zuma have to be reinstated.[13] Added to this is the government's appeal of the court ruling that the decision to allow Sudanese president Omar al-Bashir – indicted by the International Criminal Court for masterminding the atrocities in Darfur – to visit South Africa in 2015 was illegal.[14] Despite a failed bid to convince the courts otherwise, the government still maintains it did not err in this matter, and instead labelled the judiciary as being 'problematic'.[15] Is this proper conduct in an open democracy? It appears to be a sinister move, one that effectively puts judges and the entire judiciary under

12 *City Press*, 'Govt review will include appeals court', News24, 27 March 2012. Available at www.news24.com. Accessed on 14 August 2016.
13 Genevieve Quintal and Naledi Shange, 'Zuma should face criminal charges, court says', News24, 29 April 2016. Available at www.news24.com. Accessed on 12 August 2016.
14 Qaanitah Hunter, Mmanaledi Mataboge and Phillip de Wet, 'How Zuma and minister plotted Omar al-Bashir's escape', *Mail & Guardian*, 19 June 2015. Available at mg.co.za. Accessed on 27 July 2016.
15 eNCA, 'Gwede Mantashe criticises judiciary as being problematic', 23 June 2015. Available at www.enca.co.za. Accessed on 27 July 2016.

pressure. The executive under Zuma is extremely litigious, and in most cases it has no defensible principle upon which to base its court challenges. When the government decides to take the legal route, it often loses in court because the legislation upon which its actions are based is so poorly drafted. The situation is further exacerbated by poor legal advice.

A government review of court decisions will lead to conclusions being drawn on how these decisions have interfered with the executive in carrying out its political mandate. There is just no way the government could have good intentions in carrying out this type of review.

According to the principle of separation of powers, the executive or Cabinet have no business in creating an uncomfortable environment for the courts to carry out their function. But it is the trump card for any ruling party to intimidate judges by labelling their decisions as running counter to the mandate of the party. In the parlance of South African politics, the judges are often referred to as 'counter-revolutionary'.[16] This is how politicians throw the judiciary straight into the dungeon of public opinion, knowing that judges have no means to defend themselves in open public forums, because they usually prefer not to take part in such discussions – particularly where their decisions are criticised. It is therefore convenient for a government that has not done well in achieving its grand goals of transformation to shift the blame to the defenceless judges. This is the context to the Zuma administration's decision to review judicial decisions.[17]

---

16 Paul Hoffmann, 'All judges who are true to their oath of office are counter-revolutionaries', *Rand Daily Mail*, 27 August 2015. Available at www.rdm.co.za. Accessed on 27 July 2016.

17 Eythan Morris, 'A Review of Concourt and SCA Decisions: Undermining or Empowering the Rule of Law?', Helen Suzman Foundation, 6 September 2013. Available at www.hsf.org.za. Accessed on 27 July 2016.

A comprehensive review of the decisions of the courts is utterly sinister. It is an exercise that any well-meaning government should avoid. It should be left to academics and researchers to carry out this job, with the aim of understanding the development of the courts over time rather than to pre-empt future engagements. The review of court rulings is, however, of critical political importance for the ANC government, and says much about the specific way the ANC relates to its core voters. The idea of reviewing court rulings clearly comes against the backdrop of an environment in which the ANC government perceives itself to be under siege from judges, who are often referred to as not even being demo-cratically elected.

In the vulgar parlance of South African politics, the question often asked is this: how dare judges make decisions that challenge the political mandate that the voters handed the ANC? This goes against the grain of the principle of ensuring that there are checks and balances to prevent the government abusing its power. The exercise of power by the executive in government must at all times be subjected to some form of control, even if that power is assumed to be used in the public interest. The role of the courts or the judiciary is to ensure that politicians exercise their powers or mandate within the reasonable limits of the law. After all, South Africa is a constitutional democracy, and not even a democrati-cally elected government, with more than 60 per cent of the vote, should be trusted to resist the temptation to abuse power.

At its core, the ANC does believe in the separation of powers, and in the idea of checks and balances on how power is exercised by government. After all, the ANC was a significant role player in drafting South Africa's Interim Constitution during negotiations for the end of apartheid, and in the final Constitution of 1996.

That said, the party is deeply irritated[18] with the actual process whereby the courts exercise checks and balances on government. The party is in principle committed to the independence of the courts, but it seems to have misgivings whenever such independence is expressed, such as when the courts find the conduct of some government officials to be lacking in soundness. The ANC has a peculiar way of expressing its frustration with the court's decisions, particularly when the government's conduct is deemed unconstitutional.

When the court does not rule in favour of the government, the ANC actively seeks to win over public opinion against the judiciary by labelling the judiciary and their interpretation of the law as being the main obstacle to full transformation in the country. A good example of this can be seen in relation to the ongoing debate over the slow pace of the land redistribution programme. Quite often, the ANC will point to the compromises made in the Constitution as hindering the full transformation of the economy. This is not an amateur's game; it is a diligent work of art – the art of playing the blame game.

By pointing a finger at judges as being too distant from the reality of inequality in South Africa, the ANC government can shift the debate away from its responsibility to formulate effective policy – to bring about land redistribution, for example. This means that the party's policy shortfalls can be seen as stemming from constitutional blockages.

The ANC's attack on the judiciary and unfairly blaming the constitutional compromise for policy shortfalls is reminiscent of

18 *The Times* Editorial, 'ANC increasingly resentful of independent judiciary', TimesLive, 24 June 2015. Available at www.timeslive.co.za. Accessed on 27 July 2016.

the manner in which the party relates to its core voters. The ANC has an enviable history as the leader of the liberation movement – the party that fought against the institutional machinery of apartheid. The collapse of the apartheid regime and the installation of democracy in 1994 did not mean the ANC would cease to resort to the rhetoric of a liberation movement. The party has at times been tempted to use such rhetoric to explain how its efforts at building a better South Africa are undermined by institutions that seek to protect the interests of big business and the wealthy few.

When a political party gains power by winning elections, the party then begins to identify with the formal institutions through which the party governs – for example, the courts, parliament and Cabinet. The ANC government, at times including representatives of other parties, has been identifying and interacting with those institutions since the first democratic elections. Instead of taking responsibility when some of the institutions display shortfalls, the ANC, at times, casts itself as a progressive political party pitted against institutions that protect the interests of the few and that are opposed to transformation. This is when the ANC plays the 'outsider' card. The party explains its policy shortfalls by pointing to the very institutions of democracy that it became part of when it formed the government.

For example, the Constitution and the courts are institutions of democracy, and a governing party has an obligation to defend those institutions as legitimate contributors to the overall strength of democracy, irrespective of confrontations that might emerge between some of those institutions and Cabinet. However, when the ANC is confronted with having to concede its policy failures, the party then reneges on its obligation to defend the institutions of democracy, and lays the blame for policy failure on the functioning of those institutions. In the eyes of those who voted for the party, the ANC then appears as a victim of institutions whose function is not to facilitate transformation. In this way, the party is conveniently forgiven for policy shortfalls and no longer needs to explain why it has failed to use its hold on power effectively to attain certain goals. It is politically convenient for the ANC to quarrel with the judiciary, because this quarrel serves to mend the relationship between the party and its voters.

Jacob Zuma added a new ingredient by bringing his personal problems into the mix. The president finds himself having to defend himself in the courts on allegations of corruption.[19] Throughout his first term in office he had to fight to ensure that the corruption charges against him were not reinstated. This was a task that required he ensure the appointment of a friendly chief prosecutor. The appointment of Menzi Simelane to lead the NPA was also consistent with Zuma's plan to ensure that the prosecuting authority was led by an 'executive-minded' head. The suspicion that Zuma has stuffed the NPA with his allies is strengthened by the continued presence of Advocate Nomgcobo Jiba as the deputy NDPP, even after the court stated that she lied under oath.[20] Fulfilling this task required that Zuma take a glum view of the judiciary, using the state machinery to attack the courts and ensuring that the NPA was in line with his battle plan.

The judiciary has been the victim of the ANC's scheme of political expediency, which could undermine the integrity of the institutions of democracy. When a governing party develops a habit

19 Agence France-Presse, 'South African court rules Jacob Zuma can be charged over corruption', *The Guardian*, 24 June 2016. Available at www. guardian.co.uk. Accessed on 20 July 2016.

20 Jenni Evans, 'Why the DA is after the NPA's Nomgcobo Jiba', TimesLive, 2 February 2016. Available at www.timeslive.co.za. Accessed on 12 August 2016.

of questioning the integrity of institutions whenever its decisions are overruled in the courts or other institutions, such a party runs the risk of undermining the integrity of institutions of democracy. Selective criticisms of the decisions of the courts by the ANC may unintentionally create an environment in which the entire judiciary ceases to enjoy legitimacy in the eyes of the general public.

By undermining the legitimacy of institutions such as the judiciary, the ANC is shooting itself in the foot. Why? Because for the party in government to be effective in policy implementation, it requires that citizens recognise institutions of government as being legitimate, including the judiciary. By lampooning the judiciary as an institution that refuses to play a role in transformation, the ANC risks creating a situation in which all formal institutions of government are viewed by citizens as essentially useless. If institutions such as the judiciary do not enjoy a wider legitimacy in the eyes of the general public, it becomes difficult for the ANC government to utilise these institutions to implement policies and enforce the law. In a democratic setting such as ours, policies can only be implemented through institutions that enjoy wider legitimacy. Legitimacy allows for people to respect the decisions made and implemented through institutions, and also to understand that decisions implemented through such institutions are seen as capable of achieving the desired goals.

Where institutional legitimacy is on the decline, citizens often respond to policy implementation by vandalising efforts that are put into place to better their lives. Successful policy implementation does not start and end with devising good policy; it is also a matter of ensuring that there exists a favourable environment of trust in which policies that are implemented are believed to have the potential of succeeding in improving the lives of many. This cannot be achieved when the institutions through which policy is implemented and evaluated are seen as illegitimate and evil. This problem is more serious in the context of South Africa, where the relationship between citizens and institutions of democracy is still in its formative stages.

The rhetoric of undermining the formal institutions of government could deliver short-term political benefits in the form of saving political parties from taking responsibility for their policy failures. However well expressed, this rhetoric will not be useful in helping with policy implementation. Successful policy requires implementation by formal government institutions. The ANC's quarrels with the judiciary are, ultimately, not beneficial to strengthening democratic institutions in South Africa. For political parties in a democratic setting, the judiciary may seem to be an intrusion on the exercise of the political mandate to govern. However, what is not taken into consideration is that, as a branch of government, the judiciary also contributes towards policy implementation because the courts sharpen and reformulate the way government policy is implemented.

The relationship between Cabinet and the judiciary has been tense under Zuma's presidency, and judges have questioned the exercise of executive power on a number of occasions. Even when judges are not dealing with actual cases in which they have to decide on the soundness of government decisions, they find it difficult to remain silent about the wide-ranging powers of the president, a situation that has undoubtedly arisen because of Zuma's poor decision-making.

Retired deputy Chief Justice Moseneke raised concerns about the powers of the president to make certain appointments, stating that the president has too much power in this area. An interesting example of this concentration of power can be seen in relation to the president's appointment of the NDPP. The courts invalidated the appointment of Menzi Simelane. Zuma then appointed Mxolisi Nxasana as the head of prosecutions, but this also proved to be a difficult decision. After the appointment, revelations emerged that Nxasana had failed his security clearance; he had not revealed that he had been acquitted of murder charges in his youth.

The president should have done his homework more thoroughly before publicly announcing Nxasana's appointment. Had he done so, he might have continued looking for a more suitable candidate instead of settling for Nxasana. This could have been a genuine mistake by the president, who was under pressure to fill the post of NDPP, but it seems that Zuma just can't get it right when it comes to making important judicial appointments. Suspicions over the decision to appoint Nxasana soon started to surface. Perhaps Zuma wanted someone he could conveniently remove when the need arose?

After his appointment, Nxasana went to work, going after perceived Zuma loyalists within the NPA and police service. He enthusiastically went after Nomgcobo Jiba, who is seen as Zuma's gatekeeper within the NPA. Jiba was accused of lying under oath in relation to investigations into KwaZulu-Natal Hawks boss Johan Booysen. Nxasana wanted to prosecute Jiba.

Nxasana was also proactive in pursuing charges against the controversial Richard Mdluli, Zuma's ally in the police crime intelligence service. Following the DA's efforts to have murder charges reinstated against Mdluli, Nxasana followed up on the court's ruling that Mdluli should be charged. All this must have upset Zuma, as Nxasana was gaining legitimacy as an independent prosecutor, despite his failed security clearance.

Nxasana became an instant hero, and for a moment was worthy of his position – until Zuma appointed a commission of inquiry into his fitness to hold office. The president attempted to fire

Nxasana on the basis of his failed security clearance, but Nxasana was already well into the job and working very hard to win public sympathy against his possible sacking. By his willingness to prosecute Zuma's friends, Nxasana sent the message that he was not one of the president's men and was willing to prove it. This would help him to stay in the job, because critical observers would overlook his controversial past in the interest of having a prosecutor willing to go against the powerful. The fight between Zuma and Nxasana almost reached the courts, as Nxasana approached the court to stop Zuma from suspending him. Finally, Nxasana was given a settlement package and quietly left the job in May 2015. This gave Zuma a chance to appoint someone who could play a role in helping him in his long-drawn-out fight against the justice system.

Two of Zuma's NDPP appointments ended up in court, with judges having to decide whether the president had done the right job in appointing particular individuals to the NPA. The ANC has characterised this trend as 'law-fare', where all conflicts are taken to the judiciary. The question is this: what would be the most appropriate path when the internal processes and independence of other institutions have been eroded? The courts remain democracy's last line of defence, as we have seen with the Nkandla scandal.

Zuma's appointment of Shaun Abrahams to the post of NDPP also did not do much to dispel the notion that the president only wants his loyalists in charge of the NPA. Under Abrahams, the NPA appealed to the Constitutional Court in July 2016, attempting to make a case that Zuma should not be charged with corruption.[21]

---

21 *The Citizen*, 'NPA turns to Constitutional court to protect Zuma in "spy tapes" saga', 15 July 2016. Available at www.citizen.co.za. Accessed on 25 July 2016.

It is because of all these questionable decisions that judges find it difficult not to express views about the powers of the president to make important appointments, such as those in the NPA. Not often does a president successively appoint two NDPPs who are both found to be unsuitable in one way or another. What the judges are asking is whether the powers to appoint the NDPP should be left solely to the president, having seen him bungle the task. There is no doubt that Zuma has got it wrong twice in a row, but does this mean no president in the future should be allowed to have so much power?

The lessons from Zuma's clashes with the judiciary are twofold. The president has managed to create tensions between the judiciary and the executive, and these will continue long after Zuma is gone. Zuma's personal style of dealing with issues has raised philosophical questions that he might not have intended to raise.

I do not see Zuma as having any philosophical views about how judges should relate to the executive; this is demanding intellectual work, and not something he would want to devote his time to. His decisions are driven by the need to fend off immediate challenges. However, such decisions often raise deeper questions, for example the powers of the president to appoint the head of the NPA.

It would be unjust to conclude this chapter without talking about how the government under Zuma has dealt with court rulings. Where the government is one of the parties to a dispute, the court's decision would mean that government has to do something – or stop doing something. Such instructions can be in the form of a court order, and when such orders are given, the government has to abide. If the government is of the view that an order is unfair or unjust, then the government can appeal. The government has to be seen as acting in response to the decision of the court – because it is unacceptable for it to ignore the court.

Judge Mogoeng expressed concerns that the government seems not to take decisions of the court seriously, adding that he was concerned about government's passive and dismissive attitude towards the role of the courts in society.[22] Coming from Zuma's own appointee, this is certainly saying something. It means that the government does not respect the role of the courts. Realising that he has antagonised the judiciary, Zuma has recently attempted an ingenious strategy to settle conflicts outside the judiciary, using parliament to undermine other institutions of democracy. The Nkandla issue is a case in point.

The Nkandla matter shows how sophisticated Zuma has become in attempting to deal with issues that may end up in court. The Public Protector's findings, that the expenditure on renovations at Zuma's Nkandla private home was excessive, led Zuma to seek a way out of this without having to approach the courts. He used the ANC majority in parliament to accept a report that stated he does not have to pay a cent for the Nkandla project. In this way, Zuma actually undermined the Public Protector without having to go to court.

In the end this strategy failed, as the opposition parties hauled him to court to compel him to pay for Nkandla. Realising that if the Constitutional Court were to review the merits of the scheme he had employed to dodge responsibility, Zuma changed his plan and openly offered to pay up. For him the strategy was to do whatever it takes to avoid having the judges review his conduct in government. He knows he offended the judiciary, and for some reason seems to believe he will not get a fair outcome in court. For Zuma,

---

22 Mogomotsi Magome, 'State, judges agree to disagree politely', Independent Online, 28 August 2015. Available at www.iol.co.za. Accessed on 2 August 2016.

going to court is the last resort, and, if possible, he will ignore court orders. Throughout his presidency, Zuma has clashed with the law, and he harbours suspicions about the idea of an independent judiciary. The biggest problem, however, is that the continued tension between Zuma and the judiciary has undermined his responsibility, as head of state, to protect the Constitution and demonstrate commitment to the rule of law.

FIVE

Culture, Zuma and modern politics

One of the odd things about South African politics is that it has features of immediate postcolonial rhetoric while at the same time showing a strong yearning to be compared to a modern political system. The mix of street politics – at least its strident rhetoric and ideological focus – and formal politics results in most people struggling to tell if the country is progressing well on democracy or experiencing serious contradictions. The fact that Jacob Zuma has become the head of government and is seen as a culturally inclined leader adds to this confusion. How do you begin to assess the progress of democracy in a country where the ruling party elects a president who sticks to his controversial cultural beliefs that he can be married to four or more wives at the same time? What does this say about the country's commitment to modern democratic values? From this point it is clear that South Africa is caught between Western values, including democratic institutions of managing conflict in society, and acceptance of its uniqueness as an African country.

There will always be bias when African democracies are assessed. We cannot shy away from the fact that, unlike Thabo Mbeki, Jacob Zuma's leadership is coloured by cultural relics. On one hand, this has become an escape route for him in how he interacts with the institutions of democracy; on the other hand, it is also a source of ridicule for his leadership. For example, Zuma reportedly said that the charges against him relating to the arms deal should be dropped, as corruption is only a crime in a 'Western paradigm'.[1] He has stuck to the position that the money he received from Schabir Shaik was merely financial help from a friend – something that his culture allows. Indeed, it is acceptable within African culture that those who have plenty should assist those who are in need. Schabir Shaik was convicted of corruption for having made payments to Zuma.[2] However, Zuma persists in the explanation that he received the money from Shaik not because he would give something in return, but because he was just being culturally courteous.

From this cultural point of view, the argument is that the decision to charge Zuma with corruption shows that the Western definition of corruption fails to recognise African culture. What is defined as corruption in a Western sense, Zuma's supporters would argue, is a day-to-day relationship among Africans. Africans are then presented as naive because their culture, which allows receiving from others, is taken advantage of by the likes of Shaik, whom the court found had an intention to bribe Zuma, while Zuma understood the relationship in cultural terms.

The contradiction between culture and Western or modern institutions of democracy runs deep in Zuma's presidency. Cultural inclinations cast a leader as backward, as incapable of responding to the challenges of a modern society. In a country such as South Africa, where those who practise culture – African cultures – do

---

1   Charl du Plessis and Carien du Plessis, 'Zuma wanted corruption charges dropped because corruption is "Western thing"', *City Press*, 12 October 2014. Available at www.news24.com. Accessed on 31 July 2016.
2   Giordano Stolley, 'Prosecution alleges Shaik paid thousands for Zuma kids', *Mail & Guardian*, 1 January 2008. Available at mg.co.za. Accessed on 12 February 2016.

not have the platform to set the debate, one becomes a pariah just for showing cultural inclinations. In Zuma's case, ironically, he has also resorted to using culture whenever he finds the institutions of democracy inconvenient to work with. In other words, he uses culture to exclude those whom he believes misunderstand him. This is his way of disengaging from the institutions of democracy, institutions that he appears to believe are inherently committed to misunderstanding his way of life.

Seen against the background of South Africa's long history of cultural domination by minority white rule, Zuma's cultural diversion at times receives public sympathy, particularly from some intellectuals who question Western values and democracy. But Zuma is also berated for his cultural beliefs. At the World Economic Forum in Davos in 2010, CNN journalist Fareed Zakaria asked Zuma: 'You have many wives. You practise polygamy. There are many people who say that symbolically this is a great step backward for the leader of South Africa to be embracing a practice that they say is inherently unfair to women. How do you react?'[3] The question had no direct relevance to Zuma's presence at the summit; however, it was asked to provide a perspective on the current political leadership in South Africa.

This is exactly why some intellectuals have become sympathetic to Zuma – as a man who is under siege because he is grossly misunderstood by Western society. As a way of defending Zuma, the intellectuals attack the basis upon which Western values are imposed on other societies, particularly African societies. Unintentionally, defenders of African culture, as a way of life and a way of organising society, find themselves in a sticky situation when they

---

3   Paul Armstrong, 'Zuma faces polygamy question at Davos', CNN, 28 January 2010. Available at www.cnn.com. Accessed on 25 July 2015.

appear to be Zuma apologists. In this case, to defend Zuma's right to cultural practice is to risk defending corrupt practices such as receiving 'gifts' from controversial figures such as Schabir Shaik.

Attachment to culture among African leaders also draws unfair criticism, as some decisions made by the leaders can be reduced to their cultural inclinations, not fit for evaluation in a modern political framework. Culture can also be used to evade accountability. The importance of culture in South African politics is not without contention. The debate in parliament over the Nkandla saga[4] – regarding whether Zuma should repay some of the money spent on his private home – also highlighted the fact that South Africans are caught between tradition (or culture) and modern politics.

The raucous scenes in parliament in 2015 and 2016, widely thought to have been instigated by the Economic Freedom Fighters (EFF), have been criticised as a display of disrespect by the self-proclaimed 'fighters'. Yet the message delivered by the party, of asking when Zuma will 'pay back the money', is not generally disliked. The problem lies with the behaviour and utterances by EFF members when they deliver the message. They do it in a way that does not show respect to elders in parliament. Quite often I have been asked to give a viewpoint on the deterioration of parliament since the advent of EFF members following the 2014 national elections. It is a difficult issue to respond to because the question is biased, in the sense that it presumes that the EFF has brought disrespect to parliament. Further, the question is framed in a way that presupposes that parliament enjoyed some level of respect and decency before the EFF joined the house.

---

4   Marianne Merten, 'Nkandla: tours, debates and still no insight', Independent Online, 30 July 2015. Available at www.iol.co.za. Accessed on 20 March 2016.

In discussing this question, I often ask people to compare what they call 'deterioration in parliament' with what parliament was before the EFF came in. It was a sleeping parliament, and EFF members literally raised concerns about ANC members who snooze during debates.[5] Perhaps there was too much respect for tradition and the elders in parliament before the EFF arrived. Enter the EFF – and it's all gone. It is not something I would worry about too much, because the 'disrespect' shown by the EFF in parliament is what the country needed: a wake-up call to attend to the fact that accountability is more important than the cultural etiquette of not challenging the status quo.

The question of whether the EFF is the right party to raise these issues in parliament is another matter altogether. It might be the case that the EFF is not really committed to accountability in parliament, that their main concern is to embarrass Zuma, who happens to be Julius Malema's political nemesis. Be that as it may, South Africa stands to gain when questions of accountability are raised in parliament, even if the questions might be raised by those with sinister motives.

There is a lot about the EFF that I think is unclear and outright clumsy. But I do think the party has challenged the whole idea of 'respect' and culture in politics in a way that says politics is not going to be business as usual.

When Speaker of parliament Baleka Mbete said to EFF MP Floyd Shivambu that she is his mother and therefore needs to be addressed with due respect, Shivambu stated that parliament is a modern democratic institution where decisions have to be logical,

---

5   TimesLive, 'Viral Video: "She's still sleeping" – EFF's Ndlozi chastises sleeping ANC MP', TimesLive, 8 April 2016. Available at www.timeslive.co.za. Accessed on 20 July 2016.

constitutional and rational.[6] There is no place to use culture and motherhood to scupper rigorous debate and the call for accountability. The words that came from Shivambu's mouth were indeed brutal to someone who wanted to assume the role of a mother to a young politician, but these are words that challenge South Africa's conservative culture when it comes to political engagement. It was a way of saying, 'Let's reason and leave out our culture and tradition.' After all, South Africa is a constitutional democracy and not a monarchy.

Some observers were perturbed by the emergence of this type of engagement in parliament,[7] and are undecided whether to tolerate such vulgarity in the interests of democracy and accountability. Pandora's box has been opened, and no one can hide behind culture to avoid being answerable to the seeming political delinquents of the EFF. The deputy Speaker of parliament, Lechesa Tsenoli, attempted to play a cultural card by accusing the EFF of being disrespectful. He said to Julius Malema, '*Ni ya delela*', a Zulu phrase meaning 'you have no respect for elders; you are a morass'.[8] Malema responded by asking the deputy Speaker to withdraw the statement, adding that he should stop being emotional and follow the rules of engagement instead of resorting to cultural blackmail.

South Africa is a conservative country, and most of its citizens are, in one way or another, tied to cultural, traditional and religious networks where certain types of behaviour are expected

6   Jan-Jan Joubert and Thabo Mokone, 'Floyd to Speaker: You're not my mom', TimesLive, 27 November 2014. Available at www.timeslive.co.za. Accessed on 31 July 2016.

7   Bongani Mbindwana, 'Parliament: Ndlozi's "mistress" slight demeans women', Daily Maverick, 11 August 2015. Available at www.dailymaverick.co.za. Accessed on 10 May 2016.

8   Michael Chavinda, 'You must withdraw *delela*', 20 December 2015. Available at www.youtube.com. Accessed on 31 July 2016.

from them. The conflict between cultural inclinations and the rules of engagement in a modern democracy continues to emerge. Jacob Zuma has benefited from his cultural inclinations in different ways. He was loved and preferred as a president because he understood and was not embarrassed to subscribe to his culture. His supporters interpreted this as an indication of his honesty and reliability.

Zuma's culture has also led to him being cast as a pariah. At this point, it is difficult to determine whether South Africans prefer a strong presence of culture in their political discourse or not. The country, however, is experiencing a significant push against the overt presence of culture; it is a rebellion from below. This push also indicates the clash of generations, whereby younger leaders are coming into direct conflict with tradition. As these lines are written, the average age of a political party leader in South Africa is 61. With emergence of younger party leaders, such as the DA's Mmusi Maimane and EFF's Julius Malema, both under 40, we can expect to see a clash of ideas when the younger crop of leaders engages with the elderly leadership. Zuma might be the last openly culture-inclined leader in the country as it moves rapidly towards embracing the goods and practices of a modern democratic society. At least Zuma's tenure as the president has produced a cultural debate, something the country should not shy away from.

The amplification of culture during Zuma's tenure has taken different forms, some quite odd and difficult to explain. Nelson Mandela was generally referred to as 'Tata Madiba', the 'father of the nation'. Indeed, Mandela being quite elderly, the practice of referring to him as 'Tata' became common after his retirement. This makes sense, culturally speaking. However, while he was still president, Mandela was commonly referred to as 'President Mandela', and sometimes as 'Madiba', his clan name. No doubt Mandela was a father figure to the nation, and he also came from a chiefly family.

Interestingly, Zuma's ministers and loyalists often refer to him as 'Ubaba' (father). I have personally heard some Cabinet ministers call Zuma 'Ubaba'. Those who are politically aligned to Zuma seem to use this affectation, which also carries a cultural reference. He is quite senior in age, but not sufficiently elderly to be referred to in this manner in the party. Perhaps the explanation for this lies in how Thabo Mbeki related to cultural references and etiquettes during his tenure as president.

Save for his 'I am an African' speech in 1996, Mbeki did not demonstrate much affection for cultural references. This does not mean he did not respect culture; he simply kept some distance between the political space and the cultural space. During his term as president, Mbeki was generally referred to as 'President Mbeki' or 'Comrade Mbeki', while some would say 'Mvuyelwa' (his middle name). Even after his departure from government, his comrades did not address the former president as 'Ubaba'; those who worked closely with Mbeki rather referred to him as 'Chief', a term of endearment expressing collegiality. The manner in which Mbeki distanced himself from his culture, or from culture generally, may have created a yearning in the country for someone who could bring back to politics a sense of both culture and fatherhood. Perhaps some ANC members wanted a father figure, a person culturally rooted and not ashamed to express it. But this has its own limits within the political space, as the Zuma presidency has shown.

The dilemma is that if the leader enjoys cultural identity and reference from his or her comrades, that very culture will render it difficult for the comrades to evaluate that leader as a player operating in a modern constitutional democracy. In some cultures, it is abhorrent to subject the conduct of an elder to logical or rational evaluation. This is not to say that cultural practices or culturally based understanding of a leader inherently stand against logic. However, from an African cultural point of view, the conduct of an elderly person enjoys respect by mere virtue of the fact that the person is elderly. If a person enjoys such respect, then their conduct cannot be fully questioned – especially by those who are younger. That would be uncultural and disrespectful, and would be seen as being 'clever'. This understanding of Zuma the person may have helped to suppress open criticism by some senior members of the ANC. Who would want to attack their father? That is almost blasphemous. However, creating a cultural enclave in a modern democratic society, with a constitution that demands a high level of accountability – as South Africa's does – is a total contradiction.

People will always come to politics as cultural beings. The challenge comes when their cultural beliefs overwhelm what is required of them in a modern society and within the institutions of democracy. For a nation such as South Africa, with a limited experience of democratic institutions, the interference of culture in the manner in which leaders engage with the institutions of democracy may have an impact on how these institutions attain shape and function. I am of the view that, at this point, the institutions of democracy – including the courts and perhaps even the Public Protector – are pitted against culture, at least as narrowly defined in Zuma's life experience. The tension between culture and accountability will continue to be expressed in the functioning of various institutions.

South Africa is an African country, and its politics certainly shows cultural elements. The same can be said about certain Asian countries, where some democratic principles are in conflict with long-standing cultural practices and behaviours. In the case of South Africa, culture is a controversial subject, as one of the instruments used by the apartheid system to oppress the black majority was the refusal to acknowledge their cultures and identities in certain spaces.

The only instance when apartheid really recognised the cultural identity of people was when it allowed for the formation of the Bantustans, the homeland administration along distinct ethnic identities based on culture and language. Beginning in the late 1950s, the elaboration of the Bantustan system, and the subsequent formation of the TBVC states (Transkei, Bophuthatswana, Venda and Ciskei), represented the apartheid system's twisted affirmation of cultural and ethnic distinctness. The Tswana-speaking people who shared the same cultural background and language were under Bophuthatswana. The Venda-speaking communities were under the Venda administration/homeland. The same applied to the Ciskei and Transkei, where the Xhosa-speaking communities were allowed to exist. Under this system, however, distinct cultural and ethnic identities could only be expressed within the separate 'self-rule' administrations. Yet these identities were not affirmed within the broader government system; the system excluded the majority of blacks.[9]

The denial of citizenship and political rights to the majority of the black population was also coupled with a denial of their cultural and ethnic being. The black identity – and other forms of identity, such as ethnic and cultural – were not allowed expression in the apartheid system. This was one of the abhorrent characteristics of apartheid, as it showed the extent to which the system

---

9   South African History Online, 'The homelands', 2011. Available at www. sahistory.org.za. Accessed on 30 July 2016.

affected the social, economic and political lives of black people. No aspect of life was left untouched by apartheid.

Ultimately, the struggle against apartheid would become the struggle for freedom – not only with regard to economic and political relations, but also to cultural and ethnic expression. When the system's survival is based on ethnic and cultural domination – as was the case with apartheid – the defeat of that system ushers in an era of ethnic and cultural freedom. Hence, South Africa's Constitution recognises cultural practices and diversity – including the right to speak one's language of choice. The Founding Provision of the Constitution recognises 11 official languages,[10] which coincide with ethnic groups, and a distinct set of cultural practices. The Constitution explicitly provides that everyone has the right to speak their language and practise their culture.

The Constitution also attempts to foster a new 'culture', a culture of democracy based on openness and respect for human rights. The Constitution acknowledges the right to sexual orientation, and by implication recognises same-sex marriage. The idea of same-sex relationships is often frowned upon when looked at from the traditional cultural point of view. Speaking on Heritage Day in 2006, Jacob Zuma is reported to have said: 'When I was growing up, an *ungqingili* (a gay) would not have stood in front of me. I would knock him out.'[11] Zuma was speaking from his own cultural point of view, yet he was in contradiction with the culture of tolerance and human rights that the Constitution wishes to foster. In the post-apartheid dispensation, the majority of those whose culture and heritage were denied by apartheid would want

---

10 Constitution of South Africa, Act 106 of 1996, Sec 6.
11 News24, 'Zuma invokes gay wrath', 26 September 2006. Available at www. news24.com. Accessed on 10 May 2016.

their culture to be affirmed by the state and state institutions. However, this demand may run contrary to the very ideal of a modern democratic society envisaged in the Constitution.

Is Zuma culturally stubborn? It clearly looks that way, and he has the right to be that way. As stated earlier in this chapter, there are many people – including some educated elites – who share Zuma's conservative ideals and cultural predispositions. The difference is that Zuma lacks diplomacy, and often puts his foot in it, while others are more calculating and careful in how they express their cultural predispositions. For example, DA leader Mmusi Maimane has also come under fire for expressing his misgivings about same-sex relationships. In sermons delivered in church, Pastor Maimane reportedly referred to gays and Muslims as 'sinners'. He tried to comfort everyone by saying that part of his mission was to love those sinners because he is a sinner too.[12] Thanks to his tolerance, Maimane won't be stoning gays and lesbians, but he clearly believes homosexuality is sinful. The justification for Maimane's stance on same-sex relationships is not cultural, but religious. Religion and culture share similar traits of dogma at times.

South Africa is a complex society, and the country entered democracy at full speed – without having an opportunity to fasten seatbelts. There will continue to be those who, for various reasons, use the Constitution to express their culture. Some will do this to avoid being subjected to certain values. They will argue that the Constitution and the state should affirm their cultural identities and practices as a way to show that South Africa has moved away

---

12 Dianne Hawker, 'Maimane, Zuma, and other "anti-gay" sentiments in SA politics', eNCA, 16 May 2015. Available at www.enca.com. Accessed on 30 June 2016.

from the past experience. Those who want to 'donate' without having to declare to the world would argue that their culture prohibits them from declaring their gifts to others, as that would be gloating. Whether that is a genuine motivation or just a way to avoid accountability is something still to be debated. The reality of the matter, however, is that our democracy is yet to figure out how to understand these issues.

Jacob Zuma has been a cultural champion to many, openly flaunting it to anyone who cares to look. His culture might have temporarily helped him stay out of jail when he was accused of receiving gifts from a man whom the court said intended to corrupt him. Maybe we will never know whether Zuma received money from Schabir Shaik on the understanding that his culture allows him to receive and be grateful, or whether his culture came in handy as a way to explain a sticky situation. Whichever version one chooses to believe, the fact is that there is an issue to debate regarding the interface of culture and tradition in a modern democracy.

SIX

The new politics of disruption

Politics is about the exchange of power. Those who are able to seek and attain political power have to do so under circumstances not of their choice. Karl Marx wrote that men make their own history, but they do not make it as they please.[1] If one truly cannot create conditions under which to attain political power, then one has to wait for favourable conditions and jump when the right opportunity presents itself.

The emergence of the Economic Freedom Fighters (EFF) as a political party is an example of disgruntled politicians recognising an opportunity and taking the gap. Fortunately for the EFF, South Africa has an abundance of issues to use for mobilising political support. The EFF's slogan of bringing about economic freedom did not take much thinking. As inequality is one of the defining characteristics of South African society, it was low-hanging fruit simply waiting to be grabbed. The standard for establishing a political party, or for criticising those that exist in South Africa, is quite low. It doesn't take a genius to figure out the main policy challenges under the ANC government. Nor does it take a rocket scientist to come up with a slogan that seems like a good alternative to ANC policy.

The opportunities created in South Africa's political system

---

1   Karl Marx, 'The Eighteenth Brumaire of Louis Bonaparte', 1852. Available at www.marxists.org. Accessed on 14 August 2016.

have become starker under the presidency of Jacob Zuma. This might not be entirely to do with Zuma's leadership. Some opportunities were brewing as far back as Thabo Mbeki's term, and have only come to fruition under Zuma. But under Zuma even the most unimaginative politicians have been able to form a political party and challenge the ANC, and yet the ANC has failed to provide a convincing response. Zuma's term has coincided with an increasing boldness for doubters to go public without worrying about being wrong. It is a time when those who have a shred of doubt about how the country is run are able to summon the guts to express their feelings openly.

It is in this period that the pact between workers and trade unions has become weaker – if not totally collapsing. It is important to understand the political opportunism that emerged during the period since Zuma took over. During Mbeki's term, for example, there were indications that the tripartite alliance was undergoing a stress test; the tolerance between the African National Congress (ANC), the Congress of South African Trade Unions (Cosatu) and the South African Communist Party (SACP) was subjected to strain. Mbeki did not take the SACP seriously; in fact, he did not even waste much time engaging with the party, apart from for occasional philosophical ridicule. At times he would berate the narrow political posturing of some SACP members. Mbeki made it clear that it was the ANC that was in charge, and the party never had any intentions to go the socialist way.[2]

Yet the SACP and Cosatu did not openly engage with Mbeki. They preferred rather to topple him by bringing in Zuma, who somehow appropriated the leftist ticket. Zuma had no known leftist credentials whatsoever; he found the leftists in wonderland

---

2   News24, 'Mbeki frustrates ANC alliance', 23 July 2002. Available at www. news24.com. Accessed on 20 July 2016.

and rescued them from Mbeki's assault, in return for their support in his ascension to the helm of the ANC. Zuma was at the right place at the right time, the time when any 'alternative' would do. Alas, not much thought was given to what should constitute an alternative at that time.

Zuma's rise coincided with a breakdown in the social pact. This can be seen in the form of divisions within the trade union movement, the increasing isolation of the SACP from the broader leftist camp, and the general return of political rhetoric to the country's politics. What is also interesting is the recent deterioration of the relationship between the official opposition, the Democratic Alliance (DA), and the ruling ANC.

This breakdown of cooperation has many causes, but it essentially indicates that South African politics will no longer be defined by the relationship between the ANC and the DA. The DA is undoubtedly an influential party, and has at times attained respect and understanding from the ANC for its role in South African politics. This means that the rules of the game in terms of the relationship between the ruling ANC and the broader opposition are beginning to be shaped by how the ANC relates to the DA. Towards the end of the second decade of democracy, one could have argued that South Africa was becoming a two-party state.

In political science, a two-party system is inherently stable, because the two dominant parties respond to each other's demands. This is good news for investors, who are always concerned about the predictability of policies. For example, when the ANC government adopted the National Development Plan (NDP) as a blueprint for policy direction, most political parties advocated the speedy implementation of the plan.[3] There was no critical reflec-

---

3   Eythan Morris, 'The National Development Plan (NDP): the current state of play', Helen Suzman Foundation, 20 June 2013. Available at www.hsf. org.za. Accessed on 17 June 2016.

tion about what the NDP meant for a country such as ours. The DA favoured the NDP, often sparking criticisms from Cosatu-affiliated unions that the NDP has a DA-inspired liberal agenda.[4] This was before the national elections in May 2014. Prior to the elections, the ANC government announced a 'Youth Employment Incentive Law', aimed at giving employers tax breaks and other incentives whenever they employed young people with no work experience. This was criticised by Cosatu as being inspired by a similar DA policy.[5]

The supposed policy 'cooperation' between the DA and the ANC could, under different circumstances, be seen as an indication of an emerging maturity in South African politics. If the main opposition party and the ruling party can cooperate in certain policy areas, the nation benefits, as this makes possible swift policy implementation. The cooperation between the DA and the ANC, however, became costly for both parties. The ANC was accused by some of being a sell-out, and the DA was dubbed 'ANC-lite'. Despite the ANC being viewed with suspicion by the left-leaning trade unions within Cosatu, when the DA and ANC find each other on policy matters this is an opportunity for the two parties to lead the formation of the social pact – a broader platform for cooperation in the interests of serving the nation. Opportunity for this type of cooperation suddenly disappeared towards the end of Zuma's first term as president, and was nowhere to be found after the May 2014 general elections.

---

4   Nickolaus Bauer, 'Cosatu's Vavi condemns national development plan', *Mail & Guardian*, 12 March 2013. Available at mg.co.za. Accessed on 20 May 2015.
5   South African Press Association, 'Parliament passes youth wage subsidy', *Mail & Guardian*, 31 October 2013. Available at mg.co.za. Accessed on 10 January 2016.

Having forged a cooperative relationship as a ruling party and an opposition – as benevolent opponents – for a period spanning more than a decade, the relationship between the ANC and the DA regressed back to the original basis of doubt and suspicion. This collapse of trust was followed by a reawakening of radicalism, rhetoric and grand ideas, showing that South Africa is just not ready for 'gentlemen politics' and, further, that the country's socio-economic problems are too deep to be buried under the hubris of an ANC-DA attempt to shift the country towards a pact. The entry of the EFF into politics after May 2014 served as a major displacement to the relationship between the DA and the ANC, and showed that, without a meaningful transformation of the country and the eradication of inequality, any agreement between political elites will always be at risk of falling apart.

It was under Zuma's tenure that the unwritten pact between the DA and the ANC fell apart, and the EFF emerged to specifically expose the moral problems of this pact. It was under Zuma's administration – particularly in the mishandling of the Nkandla issue – that Julius Malema's politics was given a lifeline. Having been expelled from the ANC after he clashed with Zuma and the ANC leadership, Malema carved himself a space outside the ANC, taking with him a sizeable part of the ANC Youth League rhetoric, particularly the idea of radical transformation of the economy. According to Malema, the biggest crime of the ANC under Zuma is that the party has betrayed the transformation agenda. This criticism is partially correct, as Zuma does not seem focused on pursuing the transformation agenda at all. In fact, he has not really shown commitment to any alternative ideology of development. It seems that he simply improvises as he goes along.

After Malema's expulsion from the ANC in 2012, the ANC Youth League's national executive committee was disbanded and the League remained leaderless for more than two years. At the time of leaving the ANC, Malema's political path was already defined by his relationship with Zuma; he had to become Zuma's nemesis, just as he had been his number-one fan. Malema's prominence in South African politics, and his dominance in his native Limpopo, was clearly a reward for having played a role in orchestrating Zuma's ascension to power after the 2007 Polokwane conference. Malema has since apologised for his part in engineering Mbeki's downfall and Zuma's ascension.[6] One thing Malema has not apologised for is being party to the network of patronage he was allowed to create in Limpopo after Zuma came to power.[7]

When Malema and Zuma fell out, Malema took it upon himself to bring down his erstwhile ally. He founded the EFF franchise, which largely defines itself as a party ready to do what the ANC has failed to do under Zuma. The project requires that Zuma is delegitimised both as head of state and as president of the ANC. It also requires Malema to adopt a strong rhetorical stance on how to understand South African politics in the past 20 years. Through Malema, the EFF has been able to drive home the idea that nothing in South Africa works, even criticising Nelson Mandela's contribution in government.[8]

The EFF also seeks to champion the rhetoric that says South African politics has been dominated by an unholy alliance between

---

6   Staff Writer, 'Malema apologies to Mbeki for backing Zuma', *Business Day*, 17 February 2016. Available at www.bdlive.co.za. Accessed on 30 July 2016.

7   South African Press Association, 'Malema using Ratanang Family Trust for own benefit: report', TimesLive, 9 December 2012. Available at www. timeslive.co.za. Accessed on 30 July 2016.

8   Karabo Ngoepe, 'Malema anti-Mandela comments those of an immature dope: Cope', TimesLive, 28 November 2015. Available at www.timeslive. co.za. Accessed on 16 May 2016.

the DA and the ANC.[9] In the pre-EFF parliament, when the DA disagreed with the ANC, the issues would be taken to court instead of being directly confronted in parliament. In reality, there isn't much difference between the DA and ANC when it comes to economic policy – except in the rhetoric used. The DA's attempt to attract the votes of the 'black middle class' required that the party did not desecrate the ANC, or at least showed some respect to the role of the ruling party in society. This is because insulting the ANC could easily be interpreted as a show of racial supremacy from a party that is traditionally seen as white-based. Therefore, the DA found itself in a civil relationship with the ANC because it would have been too politically costly and unstrategic for the party to be seen to harbour doubts about black leadership.

During that time, parliamentary debates between the ANC and DA were also different. Other opposition parties, such as the Congress of the People (Cope) and Bantu Holomisa's United Democratic Movement (UDM), followed the lead of the DA's 'civilised' opposition and limited their objections to the ANC to formal structures of engagement such as the courts and parliament. The picture that emerged, in parliament and in general political discourse, was that South African politics was maturing. For once, I thought, all political parties believed in the same rules of engagement. The idea of the DA as the official opposition seemed to be widely accepted, and the smaller opposition parties were considering the idea of partnering with the DA and perhaps even forming a single opposition bloc.[10] Alas, all this came to an abrupt end with

9   Buzz South Africa, 'ANC and DA Gang-up to Fight the Fighters', 18 May 2016. Available at buzzsouthafrica.com. Accessed on 30 July 2016.

10 South Africa Press Association, 'Opposition parties form coalition in bid to oust ANC', *Mail & Guardian*, 17 December 2013. Available at mg.co.za. Accessed on 15 January 2016.

the entry of the EFF into parliament. The EFF disrupted the entire situation, something that frustrated all the other opposition parties.

The EFF has become the major disrupter in South Africa politics – in fact, the main disrupter since the beginning of democracy. Because of Zuma's blunders and indiscretions, South Africans are becoming indifferent towards the politics of disruption as pursued by the EFF. Ask anyone how they feel about the attitude of the EFF in parliament or towards Zuma in general, and there will be no straight answer. Some will say they understand the goals of the party – to expose Zuma and corruption. However, they might express concerns with some of the EFF's tactics. This shows that people are willing to try to make sense of the disruptions that have been part of the EFF strategy thus far. The EFF disrupted the order of things in a way no one thought possible, but this strategy would not have worked had it not been for Zuma giving it a life, first by alienating Malema and, second, by continuing to make glaring mistakes in government. The question that needs to be answered is this: how has the EFF disrupted South African politics, and particularly the opposition parties?

The EFF has radicalised the opposition parties. This radicalisation will remain with us long after Zuma is gone. Because of the growing disgruntlement with politicians and political parties in general, there is a space for this type of opposition. Government under Zuma lacks the credibility to make decisions that people would feel obliged to obey. It has become difficult, nearly impossible, to separate the ANC from Zuma, and, even worse, to separate government from Zuma's ANC. The result is a situation where the office of the party presidency and the president of the country are seen as one thing. The practical implications are that when Zuma and the ANC run into credibility problems, government cannot be protected from the spillover. What makes the situation worse is statements by ANC members, unwise utterances that show commitment to the party more than to government and the state. If one listens carefully to some ANC members, government is only important to the extent that the ANC is in government. Other than that, there is no need to respect government. Zuma has openly said that, for him, the ANC, and not the country, comes first.[11]

This blurring of the line between the party and government means that when the ANC begins to experience a legitimacy crisis, government institutions suffer the same fate. Before the EFF came into parliament, the DA recognised the distinction between the ANC and the government, despite the ANC's failure to really draw a line. By making this distinction, the DA was able to attack ANC leaders while respecting government institutions. Parliament was seen as a forum in which members have to be well behaved, irrespective of ANC members who at times abused the party's majority in parliament.

The EFF, on the other hand, does not bother to separate government from the ANC. The EFF's ingenious strategy makes use of parliament, one of the formal institutions of political participation, but the EFF is also present on the streets. Through protests, picketing and land occupation, the street 'brigades' of the party are used to undermine certain government decisions. This strategy is working well for the EFF, and will continue to work for the foreseeable future. It is interesting to observe how the EFF strategy frustrates other opposition parties.

By being in parliament, the EFF is bound by the rules of the process, though the party has openly defied the rules on several

---

11 Genevieve Quintal, 'The ANC comes first, not the country', *Business Day*, 8 November 2015. Available at www.bdlive.co.za. Accessed on 20 July 2016.

occasions.[12] After several expulsions from parliament for questioning the rules, the EFF has approached the courts to challenge some of the rulings by the Speaker. By being in parliament, the EFF is also able to raise some issues of policy and participate in debates like all the other political parties, that is, when members of the party do not get themselves kicked out of the National Assembly.

The EFF, however, has an ace up its sleeve in the form of street politics. While some party members were in parliament, others were busy illegally occupying land in Nellmapius,[13] east of Pretoria, for example. By being able to play a role in formal processes, such as parliament, while at the same time instigating and leading illegal land occupation, the EFF is able to enjoy the privileges of being in parliament while occasionally engaging in disruptions. This strategy allows the EFF to participate in the system while at the same time distancing itself from the failures of formal processes in bringing about meaningful policy changes and transformation. No political party in South Africa has been able to achieve this, not even the DA. The DA exists only as a formally organised party participating in formal processes such as parliament. The EFF on the other hand, exists both as a formally organised party and as a movement that takes matters into its own hands to implement quick solutions to problems such as landlessness and racism on university campuses.

The ANC has attempted this dual existence of participating in formal processes while at the same time organising people on the

---

12 Emsie Ferreira, 'EFF warned against flouting parly rules', Independent Online, 14 January 2015. Available at www.iol.co.za. Accessed on 20 June 2016.
13 SA Breaking News, 'EFF must take responsibility for Nellmapius land grab – Premier', 13 November 2014. Available at www.sabreakingnews.co.za. Accessed on 31 July 2016.

streets to push for some of their political goals. The main challenge confronting the ANC in this regard is that the party is in
power, so whatever the ANC does on the streets must not embarrass the government – otherwise the party would be seen as
protesting against itself. The EFF does not have to worry about
this because they are not in government.

The implication of this type of politics, as pursued by the ANC,
is that it takes South African politics back to square one. The ANC
as a governing party is exposed as having lost the legitimacy to
make decisions and govern, despite the fact that the party attained
a large majority of the votes in the last general election. The
broader masses still believe in the idea that a political party ought
to be with the people at grassroots level. This is because of the
long-entrenched culture whereby political participation for the
majority historically took place outside formal processes such as
parliament. Under the apartheid system, the majority of the black
population were excluded from participation in politics, meaning that citizens would not necessarily have trust in the formal
process of participation when democracy was ushered in in 1994.

While a large number of citizens participate in processes such
as voting, there is still mistrust or a lack of confidence when it
comes to the ability of formal institutions to work in the interests of the people. This is one of the reasons why citizens prefer
to express their political grievances through open protests and
picketing, instead of using formal processes such as petitioning
members of parliament and writing complaints to politicians. The
fact that corruption-related scandals have proliferated under
Zuma's administration does not help the situation. For a political
party such as the EFF, citizens' lack of trust in the formal political system provides an opportunity for the party to rally support
outside formal political processes and to pursue the politics of

disruption. It is ironic that a political party with a mere 7 per cent of the national vote can bring so much disruption to a political system dominated by a party that won 62 per cent of the vote. This shows further that the legitimacy to make decisions and govern does not only depend on electoral support as shown through votes. It also depends on the extent to which a party can be seen as reliable and sympathetic to the larger part of the population at grassroots level.

The EFF's disruption of South African politics should also be seen as part of the larger realignment of politics in the country, where old alliances are falling apart and are replaced by new ones. This can be seen in the trade union movement, with dominant unions such as the National Union of Mineworkers (NUM) losing its majority status in the platinum sector and being replaced by the Association of Mineworkers and Construction Union (Amcu) as a majority union. Amcu was formally registered as far back as 2001, and conditions leading to the rise of the breakaway union were simmering before Jacob Zuma's ascension to power. Even during the Mbeki presidency, there was tension around the respect accorded to Cosatu and the SACP within the tripartite alliance with the ANC. Cosatu took the view that Mbeki's introduction of the market-friendly Growth, Employment and Redistribution (Gear) macroeconomic policy – the so-called 1996 class project – undermined the federation's contribution towards the transformation of South Africa into a modern state characterised by an inclusive economy.[14]

The tensions experienced within the tripartite alliance under Mbeki did not result in a full-scale implosion, which instead took

---

14 Cosatu, 'SACP Message delivered by Blade Nzimande, General Secretary, at the 10th National Congress', 21 September 2009. Available at www.cosatu. org.za. Accessed on 10 July 2016.

place under Zuma's leadership. Alliance members disagreed sharply with Mbeki, yet they were unwilling to break away from the alliance, or from Cosatu itself. Mbeki made efforts to frame the tension within the tripartite alliance in a philosophical manner, as indications of deep differences regarding economic policy positions, and he defended his own policy position, particularly the adoption of Gear. The term '1996 class project', coined by the SACP's Blade Nzimande, referred to the growing influence of capital on economic policy.[15] Mbeki confronted those who accused him of implementing policies that did not resonate with the interests of the people. He was never a fan of the SACP, nor of the left-leaning Cosatu, and began his assaults on both groups when he was deputy president under Nelson Mandela. Author William Gumede traces Mbeki's falling-out with the communists as far back as the 1970s.[16] Mbeki's public rebukes of the SACP and Cosatu suggested that the two were just free riders in the tripartite alliance, milking the ANC's mass-based support for political relevance.

If members of the tripartite alliance – and some unions within Cosatu – were unable to offer a credible response to Mbeki's rebukes, that meant it would be risky for tripartite alliance members and some trade unions to consider seeking a space outside the formation. Despite predictions by analysts that the tripartite alliance was headed for collapse, there were no significant shifts.

---

15 Blade Nzimande, 'Defend the gains of the working class: Take responsibility for the national democratic revolution', speech delivered by SACP General Secretary Cde Blade Nzimande, to COSATU's 11th National Congress, 2 October 2012. Available at www.politicalaffairs.net. Accessed on 20 May 2015.

16 William Gumede, *Thabo Mbeki and the Battle for the Soul of the ANC*. Cape Town: Zebra Press, 2007.

Under Zuma, however, the National Union of Metalworkers of South Africa (Numsa) boldly challenged the tripartite alliance, leading to the expulsion of Numsa from Cosatu in 2014. Numsa grew bolder and bolder in its attack on the leadership of Cosatu, which the union said had been hijacked by Zuma loyalists.[17] Why was Numsa so bold at this time? It could be that, in the period leading up to the 2014 general election, there was no longer any need for a searching moral basis for Numsa to push its way out of Cosatu and the alliance. Moreover, the leadership of Cosatu had incurred credibility problems through their close alliance with Jacob Zuma.

While the roots of the implosion were there before Zuma, it is clear that Zuma's leadership became a 'free season' – where anything goes and the moral justification for major political shifts becomes quite low. This is what sets Zuma apart from Mbeki. Mbeki made an effort to make it morally unacceptable for the unions to take bold actions that could disturb the ANC's alliance with workers. Zuma not only failed to do this, but his leadership also became so morally empty that 'anything goes' became acceptable.

Zuma should not only be understood as a person, because in reality he represents a whole system. He represents a way of doing things that has become entrenched in South African politics. Had it not been for Zuma's poor leadership, the idea that the ANC government had to be subjected to some form of accountability might still have remained a taboo. The mishandling of the Nkandla expenditure under Zuma's leadership – R246 million spent on his

---

17 International Communist Union, 'South Africa – Numsa, from red union to red party', Spring 2015. Available at www.union-communiste.org. Accessed on 10 May 2016.

private residence – is indeed embarrassing to South Africans. The benefit of this scandal, however, is that it has exposed to the general public the fact that the ANC cannot be trusted to exercise accountability upon itself. The same suspicion about the exercise of power will be carried into the future – to whichever political party might be in charge.

Further, the Nkandla scandal has shown how institutions of democracy, including parliament, are vulnerable to hostile take-over by organised interest groups, in the form of ANC MPs, for example. Before Zuma, South Africa was still basking in the glory of Nelson Mandela's celebrated presidency. Mbeki's cryptic speeches and philosophical dispositions did not offer people an opportunity to engage with his leadership. Zuma brought to the fore simple political machinations with no sophistication or attempt to mask what was happening. He also ignited a simple grassroots-based opposition style, paving the way for the EFF.

It was during Zuma's tenure in office that it became possible to challenge the legitimacy of government to make decisions and have those decisions implemented. For example, the plan to implement e-tolling in Gauteng was the first serious example of the declining legitimacy of government to implement policy.[18] The people of Gauteng simply refuse to pay e-tolls as they believe the e-tolling system was introduced illegally and without proper consultation with the community. The idea that government then wanted to collect revenue on the use of facilities that had been used for free raised the ire of Gauteng residents. The revelation of the enormous amount of taxpayers' money that went into the Nkandla project also did not help to convince motorists to pay up. Even the ANC in Gauteng province found the idea of paying

---

18 Fin24, 'E-tolls must go, Outa tells Parliament', 26 January 2016. Available at www.fin24.com. Accessed on 19 June 2016.

for the use of the highways unacceptable.[19] The issue is not merely delinquent Gauteng motorists not wanting to pay their dues, or the ANC in Gauteng attempting to embarrass Zuma and his crew at the national level of the party. It is a matter of the declining legitimacy of government to make policies and have those policies implemented and obeyed.

The same attitude of revolting against government's prerogative to implement policy was seen when attempts were made to introduce the pension reform law championed by the National Treasury. Government passed a law restricting the amount of money retirees could withdraw from their pension upon retirement. The new law stipulated that a certain portion of the pension should be invested in the form of an annuity, which would be paid out to the beneficiary on a monthly basis.[20] The plan was to encourage those who retire to save the money, instead of withdrawing the entire amount upon retirement and possibly spending it.

Cosatu undertook to challenge this law, maintaining that government had no right to interfere with how people access and utilise their pension money, and demanded that the law be scrapped. The Zuma administration initially took the view that the law must be implemented as is, and stated there would be no negotiations on the matter. Of course, fund managers with interests in managing people's money were very excited about this scheme, which would allow for more money to be placed in their hands, potentially making huge profits for the financial sector.

---

19 Baldwin Ndaba and Thabiso Thakali, 'Gauteng ANC insists: "e-tolls must go"', Independent Online, 16 May 2016. Available at www.iol.co.za. Accessed on 31 July 2016.
20 Hlengiwe Nhlabathi, 'Government's pension reform U-turn', City Press, 14 February 2016. Available at city-press.news24.com. Accessed on 30 July 2016.

Cosatu made it clear to the ANC that if the party went ahead with implementation of the pension reform law, Cosatu would not support the ANC in the 2016 local government elections.[21] Not surprisingly, the ANC made an about-turn and agreed to freeze implementation of the law. It is clear that under Zuma's administration, there has been more willingness and tenacity on the part of trade unions and other stakeholders in society to challenge government in implementing policy. Government is gathering a reputation of giving in when pressured. As president of the republic, Zuma has made it less morally costly for interest groups in the country to challenge and speak out against government policy.

Government should be able to make unpopular decisions, but that lifeline seems to be disappearing under Zuma's administration. The loss of legitimacy to govern and make decisions is one of the big threats to democracy. If a political party can garner 62 per cent of the vote, at least that party should be allowed to govern instead of being disrupted at every turn. However, when government abuses its 62 per cent support, and arrogantly claims the ANC will rule until Jesus comes,[22] it encourages citizens and interest groups to ignore the political mandate held by government.

South Africans are becoming accustomed to appreciating the politics of disruption, largely propagated by the EFF. The ANC under Zuma has lowered the moral bar to a point where disruption becomes acceptable. There are certain ways of winning political victories that should not become too common in a democracy.

---

21 Linda Ensor and Natasha Marrian, 'Cosatu threatens ANC on elections', *Business Day*, 14 January 2016. Available at www.bdlive.co.za. Accessed on 30 July 2016.

22 News24, 'Zuma repeats that ANC will rule until Jesus comes', *Mail & Guardian*, 5 July 2016. Available at mg.co.za. Accessed on 30 July 2016.

Consider, for example, the victory attained by the university students through the #FeesMustFall campaign.[23] If it only took students pushing through the gates of parliament for the government to concede a zero fee increase at universities for the 2016 academic year, then this implies that the best way to secure goals is to disrupt. This experience also shows that South African politics, at least formal politics through parliamentary engagement, is not functioning properly. Why did the political parties represented in parliament not take up the complaint by the students and resolve it before the issue was taken to the streets?

Zuma and the ANC have vandalised democracy and the country's institutions to a great extent, and the consequences will remain for a long time to come. Even if Zuma is replaced by a more credible and respectable leader soon, it will take many years – or even decades – for South African politics to recover and stabilise. This will be a significant part of Zuma's legacy – democratic institutions that lack the credibility to carry out their functions.

---

23 Simon Allison, 'South African students score tuition fee protest victory', *The Guardian*, 23 October 2015. Available at www.theguardian.com. Accessed on 31 July 2016.

SEVEN

Firepools and lies

In my work as a policy analyst at the National Treasury, one of the issues I became familiar with was a process called 'budget gaming'. This happens when a department requests a budget from the Treasury and states that the money will be spent on item A, for example installing water pipes, when the intention from the start is to eventually shift the money to a completely different item or project, such as renovating the president's private residence. Naturally there is a reason why a department would avoid stating openly that the money requested is meant to renovate the president's private house. The department knows that if it tells the truth, there is a real risk that people will start asking questions about the justification for spending an enormous amount of money on the president's private house, especially in light of the service delivery backlog in the country.

To avoid all these tricky questions, which are often asked in an open democracy, the department cleverly requests money for another purpose, such as renovating a police station. Once the budget is approved by parliament – as money meant to renovate a police station in Carletonville[1] – the department diverts the

---

1   Lance Claasen and Pitso Molemane, 'Nkandla "robs" Gauteng residents – Carletonville's loss is Zuma's gain, report reveals', *Sowetan*, 15 November 2015. Available at www.sowetanlive.co.za. Accessed on 20 June 2016.

money to its real destination: to renovate the president's private home. Shifting money from one spending programme to another is not illegal; the Public Finance Management Act allows for the shifting of 8 per cent of one programme budget to another programme. The process of shifting funds from one programme to another is called 'virement' (from the French verb *virer*, meaning 'to turn'); thus you vire the funds.

Soon there are problems of cost overruns as greedy contractors realise that the door of the safe has been left ajar. The department goes back to the Treasury and requests more funds, but does not mention that the funds are actually meant for the renovation of the president's homestead. The money is then sent to renovate the president's home. The bill gets larger and larger as the scope of construction grows, and soon the media start to ask uncomfortable questions. Government becomes too confident about its own lies, and maintains that all is above board. The government lies about the same issue for more than four years, until the Constitutional Court slaps the president, parliament and the executive on the wrist and rules that the president has to pay back (some of) the money. And before you know it, you have something like the Nkandla saga, where R246 million was spent on renovating the president's private home.

In the Nkandla case, various government departments colluded to channel millions of rands of taxpayers' money to a single project. They deliberately did it this way to ensure that once the money was spent it could not easily be traced. If it was traceable and detectable, the mess could have been stopped much earlier. The money came via various government departments, in bits and pieces. For this reason, it was not easy to detect that an enormous amount of money was being spent on the project. It was only when journalists from the *Mail & Guardian*[2] stumbled upon the Nkandla building project that the picture started to emerge that R65 million (the original estimated expenditure) was being spent on construction. Had it not been for that chance visit, the system of accountability might never have picked up that large sums of money had been leaving state coffers, through various departmental budgets, for a single project. This system would never have detected that the amount totalled an enormous R246 million.

It is clear that the National Treasury's system of ensuring that departments fully account for how they use budgeted funds failed to detect the expenditure on Nkandla when it happened – either that or the Treasury did not openly object to the expenditure. The scheme that was used to channel money towards Nkandla was an ingenious one, and it eluded the Treasury. If the Treasury had known about the Nkandla expenditure when it happened, the department could have stopped it, or at least raised a red flag. If the Treasury knew and there was no need to raise questions because the expenditure was not suspicious at the outset, then the subsequent cost escalations should have pushed the Treasury to openly ask questions or even to leak the details of the expenditure.

The only explanation regarding the total silence of the National Treasury about Nkandla is that the department could not detect the expenditure. This is clearly because the project was conceived in such a way that it would evade detection. The project cost was spread across different departments, and all those departments engaged in budget gaming. Clearly there was an intention to deceive.

That this web of lies, which has come to be known as Nkandla-gate, spans many government departments is clear. Some of the

---

2   Chris Roper, 'The day we broke Nkandla', *Mail & Guardian*, 4 December 2013. Available at mg.co.za. Accessed on 31 July 2016.

departments involved are traditionally known not to be in favour of openly accounting to the public about their functions. The departments involved are Police, Public Works, State Security, Defence and Military Veterans as well as National Treasury. One would imagine that at least one of these departments would have raised concerns about the cost of the project. That did not happen, because the various departments were brought together on the Nkandla project with the aim of decentralising the project and ensuring that it did not attract public attention.

Nkandla is a saga that involved too many government institutions, and too many arms of the state. The executive branch of government (i.e. government departments) and the legislature (parliament) were complicit in covering up the Nkandla saga. Out of the three arms of government, only the judiciary refused to play ball.

In terms of the number of departments involved, Nkandla attracted more participants than the 1999 arms deal, which involved the controversial purchase of arms to the tune of R60 billion. Further, the Nkandla matter has pitted the institutions of accountability against each other in a way that has never been experienced in South Africa before. The Nkandla timeline is very interesting and warrants a deeper look at the infighting between state institutions. Multiple investigations were launched into Nkandla, some with the intention to find the truth, others with a clear intention to conceal what really happened.

The initial complaint about Nkandla was lodged with the Public Protector's office in 2012.[3] It was based on a report in the *Mail &*

3   Pierre de Vos, 'Details of Request to Public Protector to investigate alleged breaches to the Executive Members Ethics Code by President Jacob Zuma', 21 November 2012. Available at constitutionallyspeaking.co.za. Accessed on 30 July 2016.

Guardian, by journalist Mandy Rossouw, titled 'Zuma's R65 million splurge'.[4] When I read Mandy's article at the time, my initial impression was that the president was building a town, and he must be developing the community of Nkandla. I thought Zuma was pushing what Americans refer to as 'pork-barrel' politics. This refers to a situation where a leader develops only those areas that support him, thus paying his constituency for their political support. That of course is bad politics. However, as I would realise later, Nkandla is far worse than pork-barrel politics. The president was actually building himself a palace using public funds.

As the Public Protector began to investigate, government got worried and instituted its own investigation through a task team led by the Public Works minister, Thulas Nxesi. A proper investigation by a forum put together by Zuma himself was clearly out of the question, as it would effectively mean the president would have to investigate himself. Nxesi's report was finalised in January 2013. The investigation by the ministerial task team ran parallel to an investigation that was being carried out by the office of the Public Protector. During the Public Protector's investigation, she was informed by the then Minister of Police, Nathi Mthethwa,[5] that as there was already an investigation by the task team into Nkandla, government departments were not willing to cooperate with her office. The Public Protector, as she would later state in her report on Nkandla, was met with intimidation from Cabinet ministers who clearly wanted her to drop her investigation.[6]

4   Mandy Rossouw, 'Zuma's R65 million Nkandla splurge', *Mail & Guardian*, 4 December 2009. Available at mg.co.za. Accessed on 31 July 2016.

5   Nickolaus Bauer, 'Public protector's Nkandla investigation continues', *Mail & Guardian*, 28 January 2013. Available at mg.co.za. Accessed on 31 July 2013.

6   Public Protector South Africa, 'Secure in Comfort: a report of the Public Protector', March 2014. Available at www.parliament.gov.za. Accessed on 20 January 2015.

Imagine someone accused of a crime asking the police to stop their investigation into the matter, for the reason that the accused is looking into the matter himself and believes he will get to the root of the problem and bring the perpetrators to book. This is effectively what Zuma's ministers were saying to the former Public Protector, Advocate Thuli Madonsela, during her Nkandla investigation. Unsurprisingly, the ministerial task team found that there was nothing untoward about the security upgrades at Nkandla. Each and every item of expenditure was found to be justifiable and in line with the security needs of the president.[7]

The findings of the task team report did not really convince anyone that the Nkandla project was above board. The findings were rather unbelievable, and no one was fooled by the use of the term 'firepool', which even prompted a satirical entry in Wikipedia.[8] According to the report, the swimming pool at Nkandla was a necessary security feature, but what was evidently a swimming pool was referred to by the task team, and later by Minister of Police Nathi Nhleko, as a 'firepool'. This supposedly changed everything, because the 'firepool' represented a necessary safety feature and thus could not be said to constitute excessive expenditure, while a swimming pool is a leisure facility that the president could build at his own expense. The problem with this explanation is that the facility in question is actually a well-designed swimming pool. Indeed a swimming pool can be used as a water reservoir in case of fire. The point made by the task team, however, is that the facility was to be used primarily as a 'firepool'. Following this line of reasoning, the president cannot be prohibited from swimming

---

7   GCIS, 'Task team Report on security measures at Nkandla', 19 December 2013. Available at www.gcis.gov.za. Accessed on 20 April 2016.

8   Wikipedia, 'Nkandla compound firepool controversy'. Available at www. wikipedia.org. Accessed on 31 July 2016.

in the 'firepool' when there is no fire raging, which is pretty much most of the time. So, there is no swimming pool in Nkandla, case closed!

The report by the ministerial task team was the beginning of the government's and the ANC's desperate attempt to make the Nkandla scandal go away. The Public Protector was not fazed by the task team's report; she went ahead with her investigation and released her report, titled 'Secure in Comfort', in March 2014. When I interviewed Thuli Madonsela in April 2015, I asked her about the title of the report, which suggested that while the president was secure he also enjoyed unnecessary comfort. I thought the title indicated how confident she was about her findings. The Public Protector's response was that reports are titled through a consultative process within her team. Staff make suggestions, which are then discussed and finalised.

'Secure in Comfort' would bring Zuma the greatest discomfort since he took over as the president of country, and ultimately earn him a tongue-lashing by the Constitutional Court. The Public Protector found that the president had benefited unduly from certain installations at Nkandla, namely, the swimming pool, the amphitheatre, the visitors' centre, the cattle kraal and the chicken run. The report also lamented the cost overruns on the project. The Public Protector found that, as the head of the executive, the president failed to protect state resources from abuse, which is a violation of the Executive Ethics Code and inconsistent with the Constitution.[9] Yet Zuma adamantly maintained that he did not know the details of the expenditure and construction.

The Public Protector's 447-page report illustrates widespread

---

9   Public Protector South Africa, 'Secure in Comfort: a report of the Public Protector', March 2014. Available at www.parliament.gov.za. Accessed on 20 January 2015.

failure within the public service and disregard for proper use of public funds. The word 'failure' appears repeatedly. The findings regarding Zuma personally were rather moderate. The closest the Public Protector came to passing judgment on Zuma the person was when she found that the president had failed to protect public resources and failed to ask questions and institute an immediate inquiry into the 'exorbitant amounts' spent on his Nkandla home.

Zuma pleaded ignorance of what was happening at Nkandla. One wonders if indeed the president was unaware of the excessive expenditure that was underway. And if it is true that Zuma did not know, is it because he is too important to bother with small details such as the expenditure of R246 million on his private residence? The president's defenders often declare that he is 'busy running the country',[10] and that this task supposedly does not afford him the luxury of following up on a quarter of a billion rands spent on a project for his benefit. It seems, then, that the president believes it is not his responsibility to protect public resources. This implies that the only way Zuma can protect public resources, as the head of the executive, is when misuse of public resources happens to cross paths with his normal job of being president. As the Nkandla project was not such a case, he simply does not take any responsibility for the rot surrounding the project.

After the Public Protector's report was released, the president carried on with his life and simply ignored the Public Protector's findings and recommendations that he should pay back some of the money spent on Nkandla. Instead of complying, Zuma opted to up the game and escalate the issue to the question of whether the Public Protector's recommendations are binding. Parliament

---

10 South African Press Association, 'Mantashe rebukes Radebe', News24, 20 March 2014. Available at www.news24.com. Accessed on 20 May 2016.

joined in the party to throw mud at the Public Protector, allowing itself to be used as a clearing house for Zuma's failure to stop the Nkandla expenditure and his attempts to ignore the findings of the Public Protector. Had Zuma accepted that he should pay a certain percentage of the cost of the Nkandla project, and had he apologised for having failed to protect public resources, he could have walked away from this with much less damage done.

The dilemma for Zuma, however, was that he was fully aware that he stood no chance if he approached the courts and asked for a review of the Public Protector's findings. The court would have engaged in a more rigorous and less conciliatory process of inquiry. The court might have compelled some of the ministers to give evidence – the very ministers who defied the Public Protector's call for cooperation during her investigation. The Public Protector did not resort to compelling government officials to cooperate; she carried out her investigation amid an orchestrated defiance campaign by government departments against her office.

The Public Protector also recommended that the president should, with the assistance of the National Treasury and the South African Police Service (SAPS), determine the reasonable cost of the non-security upgrades at Nkandla. Once this determination was made the president should pay a reasonable percentage of the cost of these measures. The Minister of Police, Nathi Nhleko, saw this as an opportunity to extend the scope of what the Public Protector recommended. He drafted a report that said the president was not obligated to pay anything for the Nkandla project because the items that the Public Protector listed as non-security upgrades were in fact security measures.[11]

---

11 South African Government, 'Minister Nathi Nhleko: Report on Nkandla security upgrades', 28 May 2015. Available at www.gov.za. Accessed on 16 August 2016.

When I asked the Public Protector as to whether her findings allowed Nhleko to make a finding on the main findings in her report, she stated that the mandate given to Nhleko was only to determine the amount the president had to pay. I then asked if it would be acceptable if Nhleko's findings suggested that Zuma should pay only R100. The Public Protector responded by saying: 'It is clear the president is not a rich man; the aim is not to punish him, but to have him seen paying.' Clearly the purpose was also to show that no one – not even the president – is above the law.

During 2015, there were ongoing court petitions and challenges regarding the powers of the Public Protector, and whether her remedial actions are binding or not. The Democratic Alliance (DA) led the pack in attempts to request the courts to compel the government to comply with the remedial actions of the Public Protector. The DA's case was based on the Public Protector's finding that the decision by the South African Broadcasting Corporation (SABC) to appoint the matric-free Hlaudi Motsoeneng as its chief operating officer was invalid, and that he should be suspended and face a disciplinary inquiry relating to his conduct, which included giving himself an enormous salary increase.[12]

After the Western Cape High Court found the Public Protector's powers are not akin to those of a court but nevertheless cannot simply be ignored as mere recommendations,[13] the government was confident that the powers of the Public Protector are not binding. Parliament then had to consider Nhleko's report that Zuma was not liable for any payment on Nkandla. In considering Nhleko's

---

12 Public Protector South Africa, 'When governance and ethics fail', February 2014. Available at www.pprotect.org. Accessed on 31 July 2016.

13 Thomas Hartleb, 'Nkandla high court ruling has severely compromised Public Protector: Madonsela', TimesLive, 30 September 2015. Available at www.timeslive.co.za. Accessed on 16 August 2016.

report, ANC members in parliament were seemingly convinced that they could ignore the remedial action of the Public Protector. In that spirit, parliament did not see anything wrong with the fact that Police minister Nhleko actually defied the findings of the Public Protector by stating that the president was not liable to pay anything. Using its majority in parliament, the ANC adopted Nhleko's report, completely undermining the Public Protector's findings and remedial action. By so doing, parliament became an active accomplice in the Nkandla cover-up.

The Nkandla train was wrecking everything in its path; this time it collided with the second arm of the state: the legislature. Opposition parties reacted angrily to parliament's decision to accept Nhleko's report on Nkandla. For Zuma, it seemed, the issue was closed, and he did not need to go to court to review the Public Protector's findings. However, there were lingering legal questions over whether remedial actions proposed by the Public Protector are binding or not. After the Western Cape High Court ruling, the DA went to the Supreme Court of Appeal to determine the exact legal standing of the Public Protector's findings. The court confirmed that once the Public Protector has made a decision, organs of state affected by the decision must implement remedial action unless the report is successfully reviewed by a court of law.[14]

The question, then, was whether Zuma had to pay back some of the money spent on Nkandla. The last line of defence for the opposition was the Constitutional Court. The Economic Freedom Fighters (EFF) approached the Court directly and requested that Zuma be compelled to pay back a reasonable portion of the money spent on Nkandla, and that the court declare that Zuma

---

14 Sarah Evans, 'Motsoeneng ruling gives Madonsela much-needed teeth', *Mail & Guardian*, 8 October 2015. Available at mg.co.za. Accessed on 31 July 2016.

acted in breach of his constitutional obligations. The DA also asked that the Court clarify whether remedial action specified by the Public Protector is legally binding and asked the Court to declare that the National Assembly acted unconstitutionally in handling the Nkandla matter.

The Court agreed to hear both the EFF's and the DA's case. Realising he had painted himself into a corner, and aware of the possible consequences if the Court declared he had violated the Constitution, Zuma made a sudden U-turn and offered to pay some of the cost of the Nkandla project in order to prevent the case from going to court. From the beginning, Zuma clearly wanted to avoid going to court over the Public Protector's report. He certainly knew the Constitutional Court could hardly decide on whether or not he had to pay without looking at the merits of the findings by the Public Protector, and that this could lead to a declaration that he had violated the Constitution.

When I interviewed Zuma at his official residence in Cape Town in March 2015, I asked him whether he would approach the courts for relief if he thought the idea that he should pay a certain amount was arbitrary. At that time Zuma was awaiting the determination by the Police minister as to how much he should pay. I think he already knew then what the minister's report would say. In responding to my questions, though, he stated confidently that he had a right to approach the court and ask for intervention if he felt he had been treated unfairly. I also assumed he was considering an approach to the court to review the Public Protector's findings. Zuma's sudden about-turn that he would pay for Nkandla indicates that he had no intention of going anywhere near a court. The idea that Zuma would approach the courts was a tactic to show strength; clearly he had no intention of testing his position on Nkandla in court.

When Zuma offered to pay back some of the money, he also threw parliament under the bus, leaving the legislature stranded with their position that Zuma owed nothing for Nkandla. The Nkandla debacle left a trail of political casualties in government, as well as in parliament. The Speaker of parliament, Max Sisulu, was replaced when Zuma's second term of office began. Speculation was rife that he was not reappointed as Speaker because he believed that parliament should meaningfully probe Nkandla.[15] Sisulu, the son of ANC stalwart Walter Sisulu, eventually resigned as an ANC MP in May 2014. To this day, the ANC denies that his departure had anything to do with Nkandla, but it was telling that Sisulu broke his silence after the Constitutional Court ruling and criticised parliament for its handling of the debacle.[16]

In June 2013, when opposition parties began to turn up the heat on the ANC in parliament, the party axed its chief whip, Mathole Motshekga. The ANC stated that Motshekga had been dismissed because he could not control MPs in parliament,[17] and that he did not quite understand the role of parliament. Not long after this, Motshekga made a comeback as chairperson of the portfolio committee on Justice, where he became Zuma's staunch defender. He continued in this role as a member of the ad hoc committee on Nkandla – the parliamentary committee formed to deal with the Nkandla project.

After Motshekga was axed as chief whip, he was replaced by

15 *The Citizen*, 'Nkandla not why Max Sisulu resigned – ANC', 29 May 2014. Available at www.citizen.co.za. Accessed on 31 July 2016.
16 Janet Heard, 'Max Silusu breaks silence on Nkandla: Parliament must get house in order', *City Press*, 1 April 2016. Available at www.city-press.news24.com. Accessed on 31 July 2016.
17 TimesLive, 'Motshekga slammed after register boob', 15 May 2010. Available at www.timeslive.co.za. Accessed on 30 July 2016.

Stone Sizane, who would face the full wrath of the opposition over Nkandla. With Sizane's entry, the transformation of parliament into a battleground began. The EFF identified the ANC caucus as a weak spot, an opportunity to expose the ANC's ineptitude and inability to rein in rogue leaders such as Zuma. Sizane, a mild-mannered, reasonable man from the Eastern Cape, the province of Nelson Mandela and Thabo Mbeki, was not quite a Zuma man; the Eastern Cape has not produced many staunch Zuma supporters thus far.

Yet Sizane tried all he could in parliament; he pushed back against the opposition parties on Nkandla. He repelled any attempt by the opposition parties to have Zuma fully account for the debacle. Sizane pushed for parliament to adopt Nathi Nhleko's report exonerating Zuma. But Sizane could do nothing to stop opposition parties from seeking a solution through the courts. As the ANC's chief operating officer in parliament, that was beyond his reach. As the judgment by the Constitutional Court on Nkandla loomed, Sizane resigned as chief whip in early March 2016. He left two weeks after Zuma's submission to the Constitutional Court, through his lawyer, on 12 February 2016, that he was willing to pay back some of the money. Zuma's U-turn meant that he betrayed the ANC MPs who had fought tooth and nail to defend him. Not surprisingly, there was speculation that Sizane felt betrayed, and that he resigned because he could no longer defend Zuma in parliament and felt that his integrity had been compromised.[18]

ANC party hacks never missed an opportunity to ridicule the office of the Public Protector, with some going as far as to say

18 Genevieve Quintal, 'Sizane felt betrayed by Zuma', *Mail & Guardian*, 3 March 2016. Available at mg.co.za. Accessed on 20 April 2016.

she 'thinks she is God'.[19] Since her appointment in 2009, Thuli
Madonsela had experienced the anger of politicians. ANC politicians had questioned her authority several times, and some had
ignored her findings and recommendations. The ANC Youth
League publically insulted her immediately after the release of
her report on Nkandla,[20] while Cosas (Congress of South African
Students) leader Tshiamo Tsotetsi referred to Madonsela as 'that
woman with a big ugly nose'.[21] When she made findings on tender
irregularities against companies linked to Julius Malema, in 2012,
an irked Malema angrily protested that he had been 'found guilty
in absentia'.[22]

All the ANC leagues have insulted the Public Protector in one
way or another. Their attitude has been that the Public Protector
serves at the pleasure of the ANC, that the ANC is the founder of
democracy in South Africa and therefore owns it. Thus the party's
commitment to democracy cannot be questioned, let alone by the
Public Protector, who has been appointed by the ANC. The idea
that the office of the Public Protector is simply a 'nice to have' is
responsible for the widely held belief across government departments that there is no obligation to implement the recommendations of the Public Protector. The reality, however, is that there
was, until recently, no legal precedent on the question of whether
the powers of the Public Protector are binding. Since the Office

19 News24, 'MKMVA: Madonsela thinks she is God', 9 August 2014. Avail-
    able at www.news24.com. Accessed on 3 August 2016.
20 News24, 'ANCYL, Cosas must answer for Madonsela remarks', 24 March
    2014. Available at www.news24.com. Accessed on 30 July 2016.
21 Lebogang Seale, 'Youth leaders slammed for insulting Madonsela', Inde-
    pendent Online, 25 March 2015. Available at www.iol.co.za. Accessed on 3
    August 2016.
22 BBC News, 'Julius Malema anger at South Africa Limpopo tender report',
    11 October 2012. Available at www.bbc.com. Accessed on 3 August 2016.

of the Public Protector was established in 1994, in terms of Chapter 9 of the Constitution, questions regarding the extent of the powers of the office have never been tested in court. If an opportunity exists for people in a position of power to choose between doing the right thing and doing nothing, many will choose the easy way out. It seems that is exactly what some politicians did with regards to the Public Protector and her findings.

This attitude was fully addressed in the Constitutional Court judgment on Nkandla, delivered on 31 March 2016. In the judgment, Chief Justice Mogoeng Mogoeng made it clear that the office of the Public Protector is not just a nice-to-have institution; it is central to our democracy. The judge held that the powers of the Public Protector to issue remedial action are meant to be binding on parties involved.[23] You either have to deal with the Public Protector's recommendations or go to court to have her findings reviewed. Ignoring them is not an option. Despite sustained efforts by various government departments not to comply with the findings and remedial actions of the Public Protector on Nkandla, no government department had approached the courts and asked for a review of the findings.

The SABC spent much time in court pushing against the DA's attempt to get the public broadcaster to fully comply with the remedial actions recommended by the Public Protector. The SABC clearly wanted to keep ignoring the recommendations on maladministration and the collapse of corporate governance. What the SABC has not done is to approach the court to challenge the merits of the Public Protector's findings.

The March 2016 Constitutional Court judgment on Nkandla

---

23 TimesLive, 'Public protector is public's David against state Goliath: Mogoeng', 31 March 2016. Available at www.timeslive.co.za. Accessed on 31 July 2016.

ruled that this attitude is unconstitutional and has to come to an end. The judgment was scathing on the role that parliament played in processing the Nkandla issues. The court stated that parliament was within its right in carrying out its investigations into Nkandla following the release of the Public Protector's report, but that parliament's right does not extend to coming up with its own findings and using those findings as a basis to disregard and ignore the Public Protector's report. If parliament had doubts about the accuracy of the Public Protector's findings on Nkandla, it ought to have approached the court for a review of the report. The court's message was that parliament had failed to do its duty properly on the Nkandla matter, and instead of supporting the Public Protector, as it was supposed to, parliament abused its power in order to undermine her. This exonerated the EFF, the DA and other opposition parties who maintained that ANC MPs were not willing to keep the executive authority accountable for the Nkandla project.

As for the man at the centre of Nkandlagate, the Court stated that the president failed to protect the Constitution.[24] This was in line with the Public Protector's initial finding, that Zuma had violated the Executive Ethics Code.

Immediately after the Constitutional Court judgment, parties across the political spectrum engaged their public relations machines. The EFF stated that Zuma's failure to uphold the Constitution warranted his removal from office. The ANC, on the other hand, stated that the president's failure to uphold the Constitution was a genuine, forgivable mistake. Again, Zuma sang the 'I didn't know' tune.

24 Staff Writer, 'Court finds Zuma failed to protect the Constitution', *Business Day*, 31 March 2016. Available at www.bdlive.co.za. Accessed on 31 July 2016.

The Court wisely decided not to get involved in the debate as to whether Zuma was fit for office or not. This is a political question, and one that the court carefully avoided so as not to be accused of overstepping its boundaries or disrespecting the separation of powers. It was a measured decision by the Court not to issue a judgment that could directly lead to Zuma's removal from office. If the president is to be removed, it should be through a political process, not a court process.

The Constitutional Court judgment on Nkandla was useful for those who wanted Zuma to go, and equally useful for those who were still willing to defend him and his position as president. For the EFF and the DA, the judgment allowed them to make a case in parliament that Zuma's failure to protect the Constitution was an offence that justified his removal from office. For the ANC, the judgment was useful in the sense that the Constitutional Court did not find Zuma to have deliberately failed to uphold the Constitution. Of course, Zuma apologised on live television, saying that he had acted on poor legal advice.[25] The ANC used the opportunity to say that Zuma must be forgiven because, until the Constitutional Court ruled on the powers of the Public Protector, no one knew her remedial action was in fact binding. The party went further and pushed the idea that technically Zuma did not break the law; he only failed to protect it.[26] Perhaps the president was looking the other way when it was required of him to protect the Constitution. For the ANC, this is different from someone who actively tramples upon the Constitution and breaks it into

---

25 Natasha Marrian, 'Zuma cites poor legal advice on Nkandlagate', TimesLive, 1 April 2016. Available at www.timeslive.co.za. Accessed on 31 July 2016.

26 Michelle Solomon, 'Concourt DID find Zuma failed to uphold Constitution', Mail & Guardian, 5 April 2016. Available at mg.co.za. Accessed on 30 July 2016.

pieces. This is the view that the ANC took to its branches, when they requested that Zuma be forgiven. And in the end opposition parties failed to convince parliament that Zuma's failure to protect the Constitution should be punished by his removal from office.

Had the EFF successfully pressured Zuma to leave office as a direct consequence of the Constitutional Court judgment, it would have been a massive victory for this young party. With their short history in politics, it certainly would have emboldened them to take more radical action.

The Nkandla saga was a major 'own goal' for the ANC. Be that as it may, the EFF has been the biggest beneficiary of the crisis, nearly getting the Constitutional Court to pronounce on Zuma's fitness to hold office. The Court did curb its enthusiasms and delivered a measured judgment, a judgement that could be used for many political purposes. The EFF's success on Nkandla should not be measured against the party's goal of removing Zuma from office. But the EFF has increased the cost for the ANC of maintaining Zuma. This is a big victory for a party that has been in politics for only a few years, a victory that the ANC handed to the EFF on a silver platter.

EIGHT

Heroes and villains

The narratives of South African politics often show a fascination with personality. In a way, as a nation we are obsessed with personality. Often we imagine our problems and solutions in terms of personalities. Think about the fascination with Nelson Mandela and how many people regarded him as saintly, almost superhuman. When Zuma came to power, he was seen as someone with the potential to bridge the gap between the party and the people. This is because Zuma was widely regarded as a 'man of the people', as someone who could reach out to the people at times when the bureaucracy creates a distant relationship between those who govern and those who are governed.

The idea of delegation and representation as part of democracy essentially requires that those who are represented keep a certain distance from those who represent them. This is merely practical, in the sense that the leaders chosen to represent the people are entrusted with the mandate to make certain decisions on behalf of the people. Formal democratic processes and the obligations that come out of these can be alienating for a people with a long history of participating in politics through mass movements and resistance. The apartheid regime did not really allow for representation as a way of taking issues forward. Events such as the 1976 Soweto uprising were organic events in which people took to the streets. This is worlds apart from formal representation, where people defer to their leaders to take issues forward.

In a situation such as this, what thrive are personality cults, in which individuals symbolise the strength to take on the system. The individuals who take on such roles, however, are not seen as representatives of the system; they are rather seen as alternatives. If one does not support the system, one can engage with the system through an alternative figure, through a personality.

When South Africans began to experience the problem of alienation from the democratic system,[1] and its demand for the delegation of responsibilities to leaders while using the same system to hold the leaders to account, the nation attempted to resolve the stalemate by creating an alternative to the system. Zuma came in as that alternative. At the beginning of his first term in office (2009–2014), it seemed as if many people were prepared to give him the benefit of the doubt, hoping that he would lead well and become more responsive to the people, despite his lack of formal education. At the time there were relatively few Zuma detractors. But towards the end of his first term, it was becoming clear that Zuma was turning into a liability, and some were forthright in their view that he should not seek a second term as the president of the ANC. This was around 2012, when the ANC was due to elect its new leadership at its national conference in Mangaung.

At this time, just three years into his first term as president of the country, Zuma began to experience headwinds within the ANC. Former allies, such as Julius Malema, turned against him, and began to question his commitment to delivery and taking South Africa forward. The ANC Youth League under Malema had begun to flex its muscles and demand certain policy directions from the Zuma government. Among the league's demands were the fast-

1   Robert Mates and Samantha Richmond, 'Are South African youth really a "ticking time bomb"?' Working Paper No. 152, 2015. Available at www. afrobarometer.org. Accessed on 30 July 2016.

tracking of the transformation of the economy and land redistribution without compensation. It was around 2011 that Malema became bolder and began to punch holes in the narrative that Zuma was the 'man of the people' interested in reaching out through government policies. In his criticism of Zuma, Malema could not hide his admiration for the way Zimbabwe had taken land by force from white farmers.[2] Malema also took issue with the ANC's support of Botswana's 'dictatorial' president, Ian Khama, demanding 'regime change' in Botswana and for opposition parties there to be allowed to exist and engage openly.[3]

Malema was among the first to challenge the image of personality – of a man of the people – through which Zuma had come to power. He sought to replace that image with that of someone who had no real commitment to anything or anyone and therefore should be denied a second term as president of the ANC. The party instituted disciplinary proceedings against Malema and a number of associates, a step that began to expose Zuma to outside criticism of the way he runs the party. It was only then that the picture emerged of Zuma the master tactician, the shrewd politician who tosses aside allies like 'used condoms',[4] as Malema said after his expulsion from the ANC in February 2012. From that period, Zuma came to be seen less as a humble man of the people and more as someone who cares only about enriching himself and staying out of jail.

2   Associated Press, 'Malema sets sight on toppling Zuma', *New Zimbabwe*, 18 September 2011. Available at www.newzimbabwe.com. Accessed on 20 July 2016.
3   The Editor, 'Malema takes over foreign policy: Calls for Botswana coup', TimesLive, 1 August 2011. Available at www.timeslive.co.za. Accessed on 2 August 2016.
4   Independent Online, 'ANC used me like a condom – Malema', 3 May 2012. Available at www.iol.co.za. Accessed on 30 July 2016.

In spite of Malema's campaign at Mangaung in December 2012, Zuma won a second term as president of the ANC with an overwhelming majority, securing 2 983 votes against his opponent Kgalema Motlanthe's paltry 991 votes.[5] Zuma seemingly succeeded in neutralising the Malema-led Youth League and had survived the attempt by his deputy, Motlanthe, to take over as president of the party. More than that, he made sure he started his second term surrounded by his most trustworthy allies by packing the National Executive Committee (NEC) with his strongest supporters. Zuma was clearly secure within the party. Now the battle moved outside the party, with those who could not get rid of him in the party taking the fight to the streets, most of the time under the guise of democracy and accountability.

The failure by some members of the ANC to remove Zuma using ANC processes meant that the only way to remove him was through state institutions, to catch him where he least expects, in the area in which he does not exert as much control as he does within the party. When the Constitutional Court ruled in March 2016 that Zuma had failed to uphold the Constitution in relation to the findings of the Public Protector on Nkandla, his detractors in the ANC thought they had an opportunity to have him removed as president of the country. They took the war to remove Zuma outside the ANC; they wanted to nail him for having dragged South Africa into a constitutional crisis. Trying to oust Zuma through a campaign outside the ANC was not going to work, but it was a good attempt.

The case to remove Zuma was no longer about how he misused

---

5   David Smith, 'South Africa: Jacob Zuma sweeps to victory in ANC leadership election', *The Guardian*, 18 December 2012. Available at www.theguardian.com. Accessed on 31 July 2016.

state resources and enriched himself by allowing expenditure of R246 million on Nkandla. The new argument was that Zuma is compromised and cannot be trusted to run the country. This argument coalesced when Zuma fired Nhlanhla Nene as Finance minister in December 2015, sending the financial markets into turmoil and the rand into free fall.[6] His enemies' plan was to galvanise support across society for the removal of the president. Whether one is black or white, the shared ideal of the protection of the Constitution and integrity of the economy was believed to be strong enough to rally enough people against Zuma to force the ANC to get rid of him. Opposition parties were in on this idea, and also some elders from within the ANC. And so the #ZumaMustFall campaign was born. The problem with this strategy, however, was that it became a church that brought together congregants that were too diverse to work together. This group was made up of people with very different ideas about political life: whites, middle-class blacks, ANC stalwarts,[7] ANC elders, sons and daughters of ANC veterans, some opposition parties, activists from civil society organisations, academics and basically anybody with a Twitter account. The marches that were organised to push Zuma out came and went in December 2015,[8] and Zuma carried on as president of the country, seemingly unmoved. Interestingly, the Economic Freedom Fighters (EFF) did not join in the campaign.

It is difficult to imagine the attention-loving EFF fully sharing

---

6   Sikonathi Mantshantsha, 'Zuma fires finance minister Nene, rand crashes to record R15.38/US$', *Financial Mail*, 10 December 2015. Available at www.financialmail.co.za. Accessed on 30 July 2016.

7   Siyabonga Sesant, 'Barbara Hogan will be present at anti-Zuma march', *Eyewitness News*, 15 December 2015. Available at ewn.co.za. Accessed on 3 August 2016.

8   *The Citizen*, 'Country plans marches against Zuma', 12 December 2015. Available at www.citizen.co.za. Accessed on 30 July 2016.

credit with others were they to be successful in removing Zuma. The EFF would rather keep all the glory of such a victory to itself. I believe this is the reason why the EFF distanced itself from the #ZumaMustFall marches of December 2015.[9] The identity of the EFF as a radical party that takes on everyone does not allow for the party to partner with others and share the limelight. Cooperating with other parties and civil society organisations would make the EFF look weak and unable to achieve the revolution on its own.

The Democratic Alliance (DA), on the other hand, seems to be willing to partner with civil society activists, and with the faith community, to achieve certain political goals. It is already a well-established opposition party that does not seek the limelight in the same way as the EFF. However, the party still has some problems in deciding how to relate to ANC elders and stalwarts. The ANC stalwarts want to have Zuma removed so that the party can regain its moral high ground and lead the country in the right direction. The DA, on the other hand, wants Zuma removed so that voters can witness the power of the party and see it as an alternative to the ANC. The DA has no intention to rebuild the ANC into a better party. The EFF is suspicious of a political victory that involves the active participation of whites, because the party cannot be seen to be partnering proudly with whites. Such a victory would mute the voice of the EFF. The ANC stalwarts want to rebuild their beloved ANC. The black middle class is also uncomfortable with the idea of partnering openly with white South Africans to remove a black president, even if that president is Zuma. The black middle class does not like the idea that white people seem to respect them only when they can work together

---

9   eNCA, 'Zuma won't fall because of hashtags, whites – Malema', 14 December 2015, Available at www.enca.com. Accessed on 30 July 2016.

to get rid of Zuma, but do not really trust them when it comes to making decisions that could have economic implications.

The picture that emerges shows that it is nearly impossible for such a diverse group, with such different interests, to work towards removing Zuma. The entire project of removing Zuma became a Tower of Babel, with everyone having different motives.

Those in the ANC who intended to use 'outside' processes to have Zuma removed have failed. The opposition parties also failed to achieve this elusive goal. The irony is that Zuma has used his hold on the ANC to push against the forces outside the party. Within the ANC, Zuma has remained strong. As head of government, Zuma has used state apparatus to cement his hold on power within the ANC. He expertly uses the state apparatus to deal with those who might be giving him problems within the ANC. This is achieved by way of strategic deployment. Those who might be planning to use the internal processes of the ANC to remove Zuma know better and realise that Zuma's control of state power means he would not hesitate to unleash it on his enemies. Those who support his cause, and his grip on power within the ANC, are openly rewarded with influential and lucrative positions in the state. This can be seen in the policy of deployment of loyalists to key institutions in government.

The failure to remove Zuma through processes outside the ANC also shows how Zuma has managed to synchronise his goals within the party with his hold on the state. Former president Thabo Mbeki did not succeed at this; perhaps he naively thought that all that was required for a leader to succeed was to run the country well. In Mbeki's world, running the country well would earn him respect within the party and perhaps even a third term as the party president. But this is not how it works in the ANC. Jacob Zuma's survival as a leader, despite the increasing unhappiness with his leadership style and some of his decisions, is rooted in the fact that any dissatisfaction with him can be managed as long as he stays in control of the NEC, who are the real decision-makers in the party.

There has long been dissatisfaction with Zuma outside the ANC. However, this has not translated into successful political action to remove him from office. He survives not only because he often comes up with better survival tactics within and outside the ANC, but also because his detractors are amateur planners who often cut corners to try to achieve their goals. Zuma, on the other hand, has been rolling out a long-term survival plan since he first became president in 2009. Along the way, he has crossed paths with various opponents with short-term plans to end his political career. His plan often triumphs because he is willing to do the work and think in the long term, while his enemies are not willing to commit to a long-term strategy. His political obituary has been written time and time again, only to be revised further as he survived. The main issue is that removing him from office is often a short-term strategy by people who set out to achieve this goal for their own convenience. What was clear about the #ZumaMustFall campaign was that the forces behind it expected immediate results and therefore gave up after just a few weeks. How's that for a long-term strategy? Such a reactive, short-term approach will never succeed in a battle with a patient, long-term planner and strategist such as Zuma.

Take, for example, the failure by the opposition parties to build a successful campaign to remove Zuma even after the Constitutional Court found that he had failed to uphold the Constitution. The problem with the opposition strategy – or rather the lack of one – was the apparent belief that one could take the Court's judgment on Zuma and read it out loud as a warrant to have him immediately kicked out of the Union Buildings. It was never going to be that easy. The opposition parties should rather have taken their time and given thought to how to translate the Court's judgment against Zuma into a simple basic campaign, a campaign that could be understood by the majority of voters in the country. After Zuma apologised for the 'frustration and confusion' caused by the Nkandla saga,[10] his allies went to work and ensured that the ANC would not revolt. Even though he commands influence in the NEC, Zuma knew that he had to ensure that no political project emerged out of the court judgment, at least not within the ANC and not across the branches of the party.

To ensure this, Zuma's loyalists engaged ANC members in structures and branches and explained Zuma's position that he did not deliberately do anything wrong in relation to Nkandla. The opposition parties, by contrast, were busy repeating the same strategy they have been implementing for more than two years in their attempts to remove Zuma. It is often said that the definition of insanity is doing the same thing over and over and expecting a different result. While Zuma's people were busy massaging the ANC branches and structures, the opposition were giving TV and radio interviews on how they planned to boot Zuma out of office through a process of impeachment. Zuma was probably quite entertained by the show the opposition parties put on about how they thought they were getting rid of him this time. Of course it did not succeed.

The approach followed by the opposition parties on Nkandla indicates how the opposition in South Africa is attempting to substitute political action with legal action. As long as the ANC has a majority in parliament, parliamentary processes and court

10 *Sunday Times*, 'Read President Zuma's full statement on Nkandla', 1 April 2016. Available at www.timeslive.co.za. Accessed on 30 July 2016.

action will never be enough to remove an ANC president. The courts are also careful to ensure they are not being used to achieve certain political goals. That is probably why Chief Justice Mogoeng said in the Nkandla judgment that Zuma 'might have been following wrong legal advice and therefore acting in good faith'.[11] This way Zuma gets the benefit of the doubt that he did not deliberately fail to uphold the Constitution. The court wanted to ensure that the judgment is not interpreted to mean Zuma has always been malicious on the Nkandla issue. That is a political stance that can only be taken forward through a political campaign. The DA is notorious for opting to focus on the legal route to score political goals. For example, the party has challenged a number of Zuma appointments, including the decision to appoint Berning Ntlemeza as the head of the police's elite investigating unit, the Hawks. But too much focus on this approach detracts from the work of reaching out to constituents and growing the party membership on the basis of political issues. A legal approach to achieving political goals carries the risk of turning the DA into a mechanical party that lacks a meaningful relationship with voters. A mechanical party is needed when one wants to fix a broken water pipe, but not when one needs a political home and a sense of political identification.

The EFF is new to the game of going to court to score political points. The party should be careful not to rely too much on this approach – to avoid elite politics, as the party's sharp-tongued spin doctor would say. The party is opting for whatever works, whatever ensures a quick victory and lots of media attention. After the parliamentary process to remove Zuma from office failed, the EFF decided to keep interrupting Zuma in parliament. Their aim

11 *Economic Freedom Fighters* vs *Speaker of the National Assembly and Others* [2016] ZACC 11, par [83].

was to keep the flame of the Nkandla saga burning. The EFF does stand out in the sense that it is willing to push this further. The risk the EFF faces, however, is that, by being too confrontational in parliament and calling Zuma a 'thief', the party might appear to be too desperate and to rely excessively on the Nkandla issue.

While Zuma stumbled from one scandal to the next and became the villain in the South African political narrative, some new 'heroes' came to promininence. In some cases, political lives have even been resuscitated in this process. Finance minister Pravin Gordhan became the hero of the markets following the debacle of Nenegate, and Gordhan's career received a lifeline when he returned to the Treasury after Zuma's blunder. The former chief of the South African Revenue Service (SARS) was entrusted with the task of saving the country's international credit rating from being downgraded to junk status. Gordhan was enthusiastic about the role of saving the country Zuma was seemingly happy to keep wrecking.

The former Finance minister, Nhlanhla Nene, also became something of a hero because of Zuma's mess. Nene admitted in a TV interview that he was surprised that the people of South African reacted so strongly to his dismissal from office.[12] Soon after his departure from the Treasury, Nene was courted by the private sector for his 'experience'.[13] While the private sector has valid reasons to hire a politician who has headed the National Treasury, this move amounts to a vote of no confidence in Zuma.

Some Treasury officials have also become heroes overnight. The director-general, Lungisa Fuzile, has been hailed as an astute

12 Stephen Grootes, 'Nene still surprised by SA's reaction to his sacking', Eyewitness News, 21 April 2016. Available at ewn.co.za. Accessed on 30 July 2016.
13 Staff Writer, 'Nene gets a new job at Allan Gray', Business Tech, 18 April
   2016. Available at www.businesstech.co.za. Accessed on 30 July 2016.

public servant whose job is to push against Zuma's attempt to get his hands in the cookie jar. My guess is that Pravin Gordhan's invitations to business talks increased exponentially after he was brought back to the Treasury.

On the other side of the fence is one Des van Rooyen, who served only 48 hours as Finance minister after Zuma fired Nene. Brought out of obscurity, Van Rooyen became the symbol of all the things going wrong. After the markets rejected him outright as Finance minister, Van Rooyen was whisked away to Cooperative Governance and Traditional Affairs – ironically, the department Pravin Gordhan had been responsible for before he was brought back to the Treasury. Had it not been for Nenegate, Pravin Gordhan might have retired into obscurity. He certainly will be hoping for a hero's exit when he eventually leaves the Treasury. Whether or not he will be pushed, I expect him to announce an early retirement before the end of the government's term in 2019.

One person who deserves all the accolades is the former Public Protector, Advocate Thuli Madonsela. The soft-spoken lawyer is always shy about taking the credit for the work done by her office. She often praises her team for the great work that goes into investigations her office is asked to carry out. Madonsela has done so well in her term that she has been nominated again to serve further as the Public Protector. Unfortunately, the Constitution precludes a Public Protector from serving a second term.

The story of Jacob Zuma's political survival is a tale of the creation of legends, heroes and villains. And in this story Zuma survives to fight another day as the leader of the ANC and the president of the country. In the next chapter I will examine in more detail how Zuma attempted to cement his legacy in the state by fiddling with the National Treasury when he fired Nhlanhla Nene and replaced him with a virtual unknown.

NINE

Nenegate and after

The disconnect between political power and economic power is one of the nagging issues that keep ANC members awake at night. It is because of this disconnect that the ANC and its alliance partner, the South African Communist Party (SACP), talk about 'the second phase of the transition', which they regard as the radical phase.[1] The idea that the political power attained in the 1994 electoral victory does not translate into an opportunity to directly shape the economic direction of the country is a recurring concern for the ANC. This is not a new concern for the liberation movement in South Africa; it is one of the central issues in the Freedom Charter,[2] which was adopted back in 1955. For decades, various leaders of the ANC, from Oliver Tambo to Thabo Mbeki, have been concerned about the challenge of retaining economic power when the liberation movement attains victory.

The dilemma that confronted the ANC when the party came to power in 1994 was how to take control of the economy without

---

1   African National Congress (ANC), 'The second transition? Building a national democratic society and the balance of forces in 2012', discussion document towards the National Policy Conference Version 7.0 as amended by the Special NEC, 27 February 2012. Available at www.anc.org.za. Accessed on 27 June 2016.
2   Historical Papers (online), 'Freedom Charter: adopted at the congress of the people at Kliptown, Johannesburg, on June 25 and 26, 1995'. Available at www.historicalpapers.wits.ac.za. Accessed on 30 June 2016.

disrupting its functioning. To use an analogy, it is like trying to take over a house with the occupants holed up inside and refusing to leave. In this case, a decision has to be made on how to smoke the occupants out of the house, without severely damaging it for your future use. While you are outside making a plan and trying to negotiate for the occupants to leave peacefully, they tell you that you have no clue how to build a house in the first place, that you couldn't even manage a 'treehouse'. While you are trying to make the case that you are now the rightful owner of the house and need to take occupation and control, mounting evidence shows that you are actually vandalising that which you have been entrusted with. And here you were trying to make a case that you should be given more responsibility!

This is the picture that is emerging regarding the ANC's attempt to gain control of the economy and direct it to the party's ideal policy objectives. The political economy of South Africa under Zuma is such that the government has basically lost all credibility and legitimacy when it comes to giving economic direction to the country. The economic fallout from Zuma's disastrous decision to fire Finance minister Nhlanhla Nene in December 2015 – a crisis immediately dubbed 'Nenegate' – revealed the deep level of mistrust that exists between government and the private sector. This moment in time also demonstrated how the private sector in South Africa has become aware of the weakness and vulnerability of the ANC government, and has drawn a line in the sand. There are serious implications from the Nene scuffle that need to be explained further.

What has become known as South Africa's '9/12', referring to 9 December 2015, began with a report on the evening news that Jacob Zuma had released Nhlanhla Nene as Finance minister and replaced him with Des van Rooyen. That night, I received a phone call from news channel eNCA to get my perspective on the situation and the possible reasons for the president's decision. My sense was that unless Nene had committed some major transgression, there was no reason for his removal. The markets reacted badly to the president's decision, sending the rand into a tailspin and the markets into panic. All of this needs to be understood in relation to how government departments are perceived. The National Treasury, because it controls the public purse, is naturally of central importance. However, Zuma's decision to fire Nene has historical roots.

Back in 1998, then deputy president Thabo Mbeki raised questions about the political economy of post-apartheid South Africa, stating that South Africa consists of 'two nations':[3]

> One of these nations is white, relatively prosperous, regardless of gender or geographic dispersal. It has ready access to a developed economic, physical, educational, communication and other infrastructure . . . The second and larger nation of South Africa is black and poor, with the worst affected being women in the rural areas, the black rural population in general and the disabled.

The 'two nations' speech led to the analysis that South Africa has two very different economies, with whites dominating the prosperous formal economy and blacks dominating the largely dysfunctional informal economy. This meant that the ANC-led government would not be able to deliver on its policy objectives, such as the elimination of inequality, unless the party had control of the economy.

---

3 Kevin Bloom, 'Mbeki's "two nations" hit the US', Daily Maverick, 11 January 2011. Available at www.dailymaverick.co.za. Accessed on 20 June 2015.

That said, it was clear to the ANC that control of the economy could not be taken by force. South Africa's is a negotiated transition, so the winner cannot take all. Economic power had to be negotiated carefully, in the interest of the broader populace. This is not the only reason why the ANC could not storm into the boardrooms. The other reason is that the party was well aware that its legitimacy, when it comes to continuing to lead a democratic South Africa, also depends on the party showing respect for the 'normal' functioning of the economy, the economy the party inherited from the apartheid era.[4] The question of course is: legitimacy in whose eyes? In the eyes of the international community that contributed to the 'miraculous' transition to democracy, South Africa's struggle against apartheid was fought both internally, by the people of this country, and through collaboration with the international community. This meant that once victory was attained, the elites that would form the new government could not do as they wished. Some say this means the ANC has betrayed the revolution, but that is not true. It is, however correct, to say that the ANC was pragmatic and familiar with the reality of negotiated revolution.

The principle that the newly elected government would not engage in radical changes, including vandalising the private sector, was coded into the Constitution and became a binding law,[5] in the form of protection of private property. It is naive to think that the legitimacy of the ANC to govern in a democratic South Africa was attained only by virtue of being elected by popular vote. The

---

4   Ralph Mathekga, 'State evolution and sovereignty: The case of South Africa', in Mcebisi Ndletyana and David Maimela (eds), *Essays on the Evolution of the Post-apartheid State*. Johannesburg: Real African Publishers, 2013.

5   Constitution of the Republic of South Africa, Act 108 of 1996, Chapter 2 (Bill of Rights).

greater source of the party's legitimacy to govern depended strongly on cooperation with the private sector, and thus on not running the economy into the ground. This was a necessity for the successful reintegration of South Africa into the global economy. The demands by the international community, particularly the financial markets, are seen by some South Africans – especially some in the ANC – as an obstacle to transformation. For this reason, the ANC government always knows that it cannot engage in a radical transformation of the economy without cooperation from the private sector.

President Thabo Mbeki often expressed frustration with this reality, and lambasted the lack of commitment from the private sector to embrace change. In his 'two nations' speech, Mbeki was actually decrying the fact that South Africa cannot be said to be a rainbow nation while it fails to address the challenge of inequality, which still runs along racial lines. Mbeki was saying that the economy is important to effect transformation, and is essential for economic integration. Although he adopted the market-friendly Gear policy (Growth, Employment and Redistribution), which he ran during his tenure as president, Mbeki was never a private-sector darling. He saw the private sector as potentially destabilising to government policy, a view he continued to hold even after leaving office in 2008.[6]

In a series of letters released in 2016 on his Facebook page, Mbeki sought to clarify his position on a few issues, including the attitude of the private sector towards government policy. He asserted that the private sector chooses to invest overseas instead of in South Africa, a phenomenon that, according to Mbeki, amounts

6   *City Press*, 'Mbeki talks big business', News24, 30 March 2014. Available at www.news24.com. Accessed on 1 August 2016.

to 'capitalism of a special type', whereby private companies lack confidence in their country and prefer to repatriate capital.[7] Jacob Zuma holds similar sentiments about the private sector, albeit expressed in a more crass manner. Zuma would not spend his time framing the problem of lack of cooperation by the private sector; that exercise can be left to the likes of Mbeki and his fellow philosophers. For Zuma, the problem with private companies in South Africa is straightforward: they despise the ANC government. Therefore, private companies would not think twice if presented with an opportunity to milk the country dry.

According to Zuma, the capitalist decides the price of bread and oil, setting the price high in order to make maximum profits,[8] strangling the poor by denying them the right to have bread. Reports of the practice of transfer pricing and profit shifting, whereby companies operating in South Africa declare losses locally while paying dividends outside the country, does not help the situation. The giant mobile telecommunications company, MTN, has been accused of siphoning profits outside South Africa with the intention to avoid paying local tax.[9] The admission by top construction companies of their involvement in collusion in the building of stadiums for the 2010 Fifa World Cup[10] is another instance of the

---

7   Stephen Grootes, 'Mbeki condemns the private sector in latest newsletter', Eyewitness News, 29 March 2016. Available at ewn.co.za. Accessed on 30 July 2016.

8   Stephen Grootes, 'Zuma: Price of bread and oil are dictated to the people', Eyewitness News, 23 November 2015. Available at ewn.co.za. Accessed on 20 May 2016.

9   Craig McKune and George Turner, 'Ramaphosa and MTN's offshore stash', Mail & Guardian, 8 October 2015. Available at mg.co.za, Accessed on 20 July 2016

10 Mark Allix, 'Construction collusion was "almost entrenched"', Business Day, 11 March 2014. Available at www.bdlive.co.za. Accessed on 1 August 2016.

private sector failing to show commitment to local development and, to some extent, local laws. Even if these companies continue to provide employment to South Africans, it is seen only as a self-serving initiative because they lack commitment to the broader development goals of the ANC, at least as far as the party is concerned.

The relationship between the private sector and the ANC has always been characterised by this suspicion of a lack of commitment on both sides. As a leader, Zuma actually has no commitment to any philosophy regarding the role of the private sector. Thus, he is not a nationalist; neither is he a Marxist nor a liberal. I cannot say he is practical. The fact that Zuma has no commitment to any ideology regarding the role of the private sector does not mean that he does not draw on ANC rhetoric when he confronts the private sector. One does not have to be wedded to a particular ideology to find ideology a useful tool to fend off criticism.

In Zuma's mind, his attempt to install his loyalist, Des van Rooyen, as the head of the National Treasury was defeated by corporate bullies: a strong corporate lobby from within the private sector once again subdued the ANC. This is the argument Mbeki would use if he were in a similar situation. However, Zuma's view is based on the narrow objective of trying to rein in the National Treasury. His purpose is not the transformation of society, but the enrichment of his cronies.

It was reported widely that business leaders exerted pressure on Zuma to make a U-turn and reappoint Pravin Gordhan as Minister of Finance after Nhlanhla Nene was fired and replaced with Des van Rooyen.[11] The significance of the intervention by 'big

---

11 Franz Wild, 'Big banks "showed Zuma his limits"', Independent Online, 15 December 2015. Available at www.iol.co.za. Accessed on 31 July 2016.

business' in the Treasury debacle was that it was the first time that private companies had found the moral courage to confront the president and get him to change his appointment. Generally, the private sector in South Africa avoids direct confrontation with the ANC. This could be because the private sector is aware that poor performance in terms of transformation undermines the ability of the corporate sector to confront government directly. After all, the ANC is directly elected by the people and is in charge of the general public narrative about the private sector. If the private sector steps out of line, the ANC would merely stop defending the sector from criticism by its alliance partners, Cosatu and the SACP. The leftist idea that private companies are bloodthirsty exploiters that need to be rooted out of the country would go unchallenged by the ANC.

During Nenegate, the private sector successfully convinced Zuma to make the right decision and appoint a competent minister, in the form of Pravin Gordhan (read: a market-friendlier communist who believes in austerity and inflation). Did the banks overplay their hand? The weakness of the ANC under Zuma created space for the private sector to insert within society the narrative (and fear) around a possible 'ratings downgrade'. What is remarkable about the Treasury saga is that even poor people began to worry about a possible ratings downgrade under Zuma. The SACP made it clear that they feared a downgrade, and, bizarrely, even the EFF expressed concern. The EFF believes in the nationalisation of all productive resources and the radical transfer of land to black people, yet the party feared a downgrade by rating agencies headquartered in New York!

The biggest winner in the Treasury debacle was the private sector, but it has to hold on to the victory tightly because it might be short-lived. Although the victory came with a price tag of over

R150 billion – the amount estimated to have been wiped out after Zuma fired Nhlanhla Nene[12] – the crisis demonstrated that the ANC is not unassailable; the party can be made to eat the corporate narrative – the fear of a ratings downgrade. Zuma even insisted that his two-day appointee, Des van Rooyen,[13] was actually 'more qualified than any minister' he has ever appointed to the Finance portfolio. By continuing to defend the decision to appoint Van Rooyen, Zuma effectively disowned Pravin Gordhan. In effect the president basically admitted that the markets appointed Gordhan.

The relationship between Zuma and Gordhan has been at best dysfunctional and toxic to any system that is meant to work toward a single goal – the national interest. Whichever way you see it, there is no way that a country can be said to be economically stable when the president clearly cannot stand the minister who heads the Treasury. This situation is not sustainable, and it will not hold.

First, let me explain why the Treasury crisis, although caused by Zuma, was not sufficient grounds for Zuma to lose his job. It was all about whom he directly offended by the decision to fire Nene. He did not directly offend the majority of ANC constituents; he only directly offended the private sector. Most ANC voters would still see Zuma as a victim of the corporate (private sector) bully.

For many ANC supporters, the National Treasury is seen as the

---

12 Renee Bonorchis, Neo Khanyile and Fin24, 'SA banks stock regains billions lost when Zuma fired Nene', Fin24, 18 February 2016. Available at www.fin24.com. Accessed on 16 July 2016.

13 African News Agency, 'Van Rooyen was most qualified for finance minister job – Zuma', *Mail & Guardian*, 22 February 2016. Available at mg.co.za. Accessed on 2 August 2016.

last bastion of the 'old' system. Months before Zuma made his move on the Treasury, a document surfaced claiming that former Finance minister Trevor Manuel was an apartheid agent and had been part of a plot to ensure that the Treasury was kept under the control of the 'white establishment' and out of the hands of the ANC.[14] According to the report, senior Treasury officials, including Andrew Donaldson, were apartheid strategists. The document, which was reported to have emerged through intelligence channels, made allegations that some white corporate moguls, including Remgro chairman Johann Rupert, were actively working in cahoots with Treasury officials to capture this critical department.

In my time as a senior policy analyst at the National Treasury, in 2009, I never figured Andrew Donaldson for a sinister character who could be interested in clandestine activities. I know Donaldson as the head of the Public Finance division within the Treasury. His team were responsible for looking into each and every government budget proposal, and for raising questions if the departments were not spending allocated funds properly. I have been in meetings with him several times, where we discussed budget guidelines and other tools that could assist departments in planning and budgeting, for example. Not once did I hear him raising philosophical concerns about the ANC government. Perhaps I was just a naive mid-level manager, sitting in meetings with an apartheid agent actively working to undermine the government, right there under my nose!

What is important about this intelligence report is the narrative it drives that the Treasury is under the control of white interests.

---

14 Ahmed Areff, 'Treasury investigates "report" claiming Manuel, Ramos were apartheid spies', News24, 21 August 2015. Available at www.news24.com. Accessed on 30 July 2016.

It is not the first time that an intelligence report has emerged making ridiculous claims; in 2007, the so-called Browse Mole report alleged that foreign elements had interests in supporting Jacob Zuma's bid for the ANC presidency.[15] Of interest here are not the comical claims in the report, but the intention behind such a report. It is clear that the people who authored the report were aware of what was going to happen at the Treasury. The report was an attempt at delegitimising the National Treasury and justifying an impending intervention in the form of leadership change. When the report surfaced, Finance minister Nhlanhla Nene's response suggested that he might have had a hint of what the Treasury was about to experience.[16] He stated that the Treasury seemed to be the next in line when it comes to undermining state institutions. This was not far from what took place in December, when Zuma attempted a broad-daylight heist of the National Treasury, but was forced to backtrack after the markets pushed him into a corner and demanded sober correction.

When Pravin Gordhan was brought back to the Treasury, the minister took on the role of the 'last man standing' against Zuma's rampage at key state institutions. Gordhan might have needed this crisis as an opportunity for him to redeem his near-failed career, which had almost ended with a stint as Minister of Cooperative Governance and Traditional Affairs. Towards the end of his first stint at the Treasury, Gordhan had waged a losing battle against maladministration in government departments. In October 2013,

---

15 Nic Dawes, Sam Sole and Stefaans Brümmer, 'Inside the Browse "Mole" row', *Mail & Guardian*, 3 August 2007. Available at mg.co.za. Accessed on 2 August 2016.

16 Songezo Zibi, 'UNEMBARGOED: Timing of Treasury "intelligence report" curious' *Business Day*, 24 August 2015. Available at www.bdlive.co.za. Accessed on 2 August 2016.

he had issued a directive that all government departments should begin to 'tighten the belt'[17] and spend money carefully. It was becoming clear then that South Africa was facing an economic crisis, and the first thing to do in such a circumstance is to cut wasteful expenditure within the public service. Some of the Treasury recommendations were that departments should not spend money on alcohol for their year-end functions, and that ministers should avoid buying expensive official vehicles. The then Public Enterprises minister Malusi Gigaba took a photo of himself destroying his official credit card. Barely three months after Gordhan's announcement, the then North West provincial premier, Thandi Modise, purchased a new official vehicle, a top-of-the-range BMW sedan, for a whooping R1.3 million.[18] Modise couldn't have chosen a better moment to demonstrate how little Gordhan's Treasury directives mattered.

It was during Gordhan's first term as Finance minister that the infamous Nkandla expenditure took place. The spending of over R200 million on the renovation of Zuma's private residence shows that Gordhan, as minister, did not reign proactively over the Treasury. Reports indicate that the Nkandla expenditure occurred from 2009[19] to 2014, during the period that Pravin Gordhan was Finance minister. Could it be that Nkandla is haunting Gordhan? Perhaps it gives him a sense of purpose to spend the final years

17 Ranjeni Munusamy, 'Budget 2014: Gordhan's frank story to tell', Daily Maverick, 27 February 2014. Available at www.dailymaverick.co.za. Accessed on 3 August 2016.

18 South Africa Press Association, 'Modise says car purchase was not a snub at Gordhan', Mail & Guardian, 6 January 2014. Available at www.mg.co.za. Accessed on 17 June 2016.

19 Gertrude Makhafola, 'How Treasury determined Zuma's Nkandla liability', Independent Online, 27 June 2016. Available at www.iol.co.za. Accessed on 2 August 2016.

of his political career stopping Zuma from continuing to do what should not have begun in the first place. Presented with an opportunity to return to the Treasury under circumstances where he would be expected to take a stance against Zuma is something that Gordhan surely could not have dreamt of. His two-year tenure at Cooperative Governance, the department responsible for coordinating cooperation between local government, provincial government and national government, was a period of unaccustomed obscurity for a man who had previously been at the helm of the South African Revenue Service (SARS) and the National Treasury, key departments responsible for the collection and allocation of revenue. At Cooperative Governance, Gordhan was already embroiled in an unwinnable conflict with local government tsars who are constantly lobbying to be left alone to do their own thing (read: drive local government into an abyss of non-delivery).

His unexpected Sunday-evening return to the Treasury presented an opportunity for Gordhan to face off with Zuma. With Zuma being in charge of the internal processes of the party, and having mortgaged that control to interest groups such as the Gupta family, it meant that Gordhan would be weakened from day one; thus he would enjoy no political clout and no meaningful support from within the ANC. It was quite clear after his appointment that Gordhan would be one of the main obstacles to Zuma's campaign to appropriate state institutions. To fight against Zuma, Gordhan has opted to fight his battle through any platform that presents itself outside ANC structures. He spoke at press conferences, and his strategy has been to galvanise support from anyone who cares to listen to his plea to protect the state from capture by Zuma and his cronies. He is the champion of anti-corruption, and he believes that this time, the second time around, he stands a good chance of being effective. However, this strategy is not going to work.

While some members of the ANC are happy to support Gordhan's posture against Zuma, they are not committed to his strategy of waging war against the ANC through the media. Senior members of the ANC who initially supported Gordhan's stance against state capture include ANC secretary-general Gwede Mantashe. Mantashe was enthusiastic when the talk of attempted state capture surfaced during the Treasury debacle. Gordhan's appointment was seen as an opportunity to block state capture, and the minister clearly cherished the narrative that he is the saviour of the state, along with his Treasury colleagues, including deputy minister Mcebisi Jonas. As the Treasury officials gained public support and respect, Mantashe made a U-turn on state capture, becoming more circumspect and measured in his utterances.[20] I was not surprised to hear Mantashe say that people should not institutionalise Pravin Gordhan.[21] Of course Gordhan has been naively institutionalised as the last bastion of anti-corruption, the knight who is going to slay the state-capture dragon.

The reality is that some within the ANC are beginning to be irked by Gordhan's growing popularity outside the party. His enthusiasm in expressing himself outside the ANC, while being deployed by the ANC, might be his downfall. Mantashe is right: people should not institutionalise and hero-worship Pravin Gordhan. It is unrealistic and naive to believe that an individual can successfully block well-orchestrated institutional decay. As a consequence Gordhan will be isolated within the ANC, and he will be reminded that he never really had political clout; he only enjoys the confidence of the markets and that is not enough for

20 Sam Mkokeli, 'Mantashe outflanked in state capture fight', *Business Day*, 1 June 2016. Available at www.bdlive.co.za. Accessed on 2 August 2016.
21 *The New Age*, 'ANC warns against institutionalising Pravin Gordhan', 1 June 2016. Available at www.thenewage.co.za. Accessed on 2 August 2016.

his political survival. Zuma is a master tactician, and since his forced reappointment of Gordhan, he has been working behind the scenes on clearing his exit path.

The idea of investigating Gordhan's role in relation to the formation and operation of the intelligence-gathering unit at SARS is another lever for Zuma to push him out of the Treasury. Dubbed the 'rogue unit' because of allegations that it gathered intelligence and operated like cowboys, the unit was formed during Gordhan's tenure as SARS commissioner.[22] Questions relating to alleged illegal activities carried out by the unit were raised before Gordhan was reappointed to the Treasury in December 2015. He denied knowledge of any alleged illegal activities by the unit, which was lawfully set up. After his reappointment to the Treasury, Zuma's allies in the police escalated the issues further and stated that there were investigations into Gordhan's role in the unit. The case was said to be in the hands of the Hawks, the police investigative unit under General Berning Ntlemeza, perceived to be a Zuma ally.

From this arose an untenable situation in which a sitting Minister of Finance could face criminal charges and possibly even arrest. There was a carefully orchestrated campaign of media leaks regarding Gordhan's possibly imminent arrest and the state of the investigation.[23] Then Gordhan went public, garnering considerable public support. My sense is that the intention was not to arrest Gordhan and expedite a criminal case against him. That would be senseless and might not yield the desired results for his detractors – Zuma

22 Matthew le Cordeur, 'SARS paid KPMG R23 million for "rogue" unit probe', Fin24, 7 June 2016. Available at www.fin24.com. Accessed on 30 July 2016.
23 Nathi Olifant, Qaanitah Hunter and Thanduxolo Jika, 'Pravin Gordhan faces "imminent" arrest', Sunday Times, 15 May 2016. Available at www.timeslive. co.za. Accessed on 2 August 2016.

and his allies. The intention is rather to keep the case alive, and to deliberately drag out the investigation with the aim of not having to make a decision to charge Gordhan.

This strategy works well, because Gordhan knows that indeed there is some truth in the allegations, but no evidence that would see him being found guilty. This scenario will keep him preoccupied and somehow unsettled in his position as Treasury head. The reason why Zuma will not push his lieutenants to take the case to court and try Gordhan is that he knows the chances are that Gordhan would not be found guilty. In fact the court might not even find it necessary for him to stand trial. Therefore, going to court might bring this issue to a conclusion, with the court finding the whole saga to be a flimsy political machination. Gordhan would at that point become untouchable and would indeed prevail against Zuma. Therefore, the strategy of Zuma's allies is rather to allow a sense of uncertainty to prevail, and to keep making life difficult for Gordhan, hoping he will soon call it quits and resign.

If Gordhan is isolated within the ANC because he resorts to an outside platform to wage his war against Zuma, he will eventually give up and realise he is not an institution and he cannot on his own continue to push against Zuma. This is political jujitsu, where Zuma wrestles Gordhan straight into retirement. In that way, Zuma has an opportunity to appoint a more desirable Treasury minister. The position of ANC members in this regard will be clear: the ANC does not like mavericks such as Gordhan, and the party does not like people who fight party battles through outside platforms. Gordhan has no choice but to resort to outside platforms because the internal processes of the ANC are under Zuma's control. This strategy, however, will alienate him from those within the party who would otherwise stand with him. When all is said and done, the ANC is protective of its integrity: the party prefers to ruin its reputation itself, instead of involving outside stakeholders, such as the media. The job of destroying the ANC is reserved for the members of its innermost circle, and no one outside the party shall taste this privilege.

The difficult thing about the Treasury debacle and state capture lies in separating the usual factional battles between the ANC and its alliance partners from a conflict based on principles. The position taken by those who think state capture is a serious issue and warrants thorough investigation has been easily dismissed as a campaign by the anti-Zuma camp and their allies in the private sector. For example, there has been a strong view among Zuma's allies that the market reaction to Zuma's dismissal of Nhlanhla Nene was an orchestrated move to undermine Zuma's leadership. It is seen as political manoeuvring using the economy. This is an opportunistic position; however, it makes sense for those who are convinced that Zuma is a pariah in the eyes of the markets.

Ultimately, this serves to normalise what Zuma is trying to do in capturing the state. It says that the state is under the control of capital and some local collaborators, and that Zuma is only trying to relocate the state to more benign hands – the Gupta family and their allies within the ANC. This is about a group that believes it is waging a struggle to retain what belongs to them from undeserving capturers. This is manifestation of factional politics, and it leaves citizens out in the cold. Citizens might end up having to choose which capturers to align themselves with. Do they align themselves with Zuma's crew, with its warped sense of redistribution of resources, or do they align themselves with the other crew, which is more sophisticated in its capture of the state, the group that understands that open, transparent corruption undermines authority to govern?

There are too many proxy wars represented in the state capture debate. The SACP's version of this phenomenon is different
from how the ANC sees it. Corporate South Africa also has its
own version of what it believes is underway. For the SACP, this
is not a complex issue; it is about Zuma's family furthering their
own interests with their allies, and abusing state institutions. The
ANC's version sees state capture as a phenomenon that is orchestrated by the corporate sector. The ANC believes that the Treasury
is under the control of this sector, and that the Gupta family are
small fry by comparison. Corporate South Africa sees the ANC as
having lost its way, with Nenegate being the final straw. The ANC
regime is seen as vandalising whatever remains of South Africa's
economy, and it has to be stopped. The challenge for corporate South Africa is that, at least for the time being, the ANC is
the best option for stability. The EFF cannot be trusted to run the
country and the DA still lacks credibility for the majority of voters. The Guptas are seen as bringing instability and undermining
the ANC's legitimacy to govern and make sound policy decisions.
Corporate South Africa is balling its fist against the Guptas, in the
interests of protecting the country. The Guptas in turn resort to
small-time wannabe capitalists, such as the Premier League, giving
them crumbs to assist the family in standing up to corporate South
Africa. This is an ongoing war, with many battles to come.

TEN

Spies and spooks

Since South Africa became a democracy in 1994, civil society organisations and activists have called for government to carry out its work in an open and transparent way. The call for transparency and accountability is supported in the Constitution, and represents a crucial break from the apartheid era. The apartheid system relied on the police and security forces, including state intelligence services, to suppress and even eliminate anti-apartheid activists. The apartheid system did not operate in an open, transparent way, so almost anything became allowable in the interests of preserving the system. Needless to say, this was not sufficient to keep the activists at bay. Despite unlawful detention and torture, including the killing of Steve Biko in 1977, apartheid ultimately crumbled and was replaced with a system based on the will of the people.

The collapse of apartheid, however, did not mean that political elites ceased to make use of the intelligence services to fight political battles. It may well be that, in the new dispensation, the new political elites are to a certain extent committed to open democracy and ensuring access to information. There has, however, been an observable fascination with the use of the state's intelligence apparatus. Having been subjected to a ruthless intelligence-based onslaught by the apartheid government, one would assume that the ANC would deliberately avoid resorting to the dark world of intelligence as a way to control society. But it would be a mistake to make that assumption.

The presidencies of Thabo Mbeki and Jacob Zuma have revealed the extent to which the ANC elites are still fascinated by the use of intelligence as a source of information. As a researcher, I believe that before one sources information through intelligence and 'spooks' (spies), one should first work with the information that is out there already. The truth about society is often there for everyone to see, and it is not hidden. But once people begin to believe that the real truth about society lies hidden, trouble begins. When political leaders believe that the truth can only be extracted by spooks, such leaders are bound to be blind to facts right under their noses. Such leadership tends to ignore the obvious facts, and to keep searching for the supposedly hidden truths. These are leaders who concern themselves with conspiracy theories, the belief that there is someone out there working in the dark to undermine them.

Zuma's leadership has fuelled talk of conspiracies and the work of agents as ways to explain his political survival.[1] But is it really true that Zuma has survived all this time because he relies on intelligence to cement his hold on power? For years, this has been raised as one of Zuma's trump cards; his experience with the intelligence services dates back to his role as a commander of Umkhonto we Sizwe (MK), the ANC's military wing. Zuma's political survival and his intelligence background have become intertwined; he survives because he knows everyone's secrets, and he uses those secrets to get people to do what he wants. Naturally, when a politician withstands sustained political pressure under seemingly impossible conditions, people tend to think he must be doing something in secret to ensure his survival.

The idea that Zuma must rely on spooks to survive is based also

---

1   Joe Brock and Ed Cropley, 'How Zuma, the smiling spy, controls South Africa', Reuters, 4 May 2016. Available at www.reuters.com. Accessed on 30 August 2016.

on the perception that he is not doing anything impressive enough to justify his survival. But Zuma seems not to care what people think of him. Unlike Thabo Mbeki, who cared a great deal about how people perceived his decisions, including his controversial ideas about HIV/Aids, Zuma does not put much effort into shifting public opinion about his performance or his leadership. He has no sense of public relations, and he does not devote much time to it. He will utter one controversial statement after another, and leave it to his spin doctors to try to clean up the mess. This is clearly someone who does not care what people think about him. Perhaps Zuma purposefully does not give credence to information or perceptions that are out there in the public sphere. He believes the truth is hidden, and therefore seemingly prefers to focus on intelligence. This is valuable information that is worth Zuma's attention, and not the type of information accessible to just anyone.

Zuma's fascination with information collected by the spooks came to light when the National Prosecuting Authority (NPA) decided to drop the corruption charges against him. In April 2009, the then acting director of public prosecutions, Advocate Mokotedi Mpshe, ruled that there had been political interference in the decision to prosecute Zuma on corruption charges.[2] The NPA's decision not to continue with the prosecution of Zuma was based on intercepted telephone recordings between the then NPA head, Bulelani Ngcuka, and the then head of the Directorate of Special Operations (DSO), Leonard McCarthy. The DSO, better known as the Scorpions, was responsible for high-priority crime, and Zuma's file was before the unit for investigation. Somehow the transcript of the recordings came into the possession of Zuma's lawyers, who showed them to senior NPA representatives.

---

2 *Mail & Guardian*, 'NPA drops corruption charges against Zuma', 6 April 2009. Available at mg.co.za. Accessed on 20 June 2016.

Some of the conversations recorded between McCarthy and
Ngcuka are reported to have taken place before the ANC's national conference at Polokwane in 2007, the conference that would
elect Zuma to lead the party. Shortly before the conference,
McCarthy and Ngcuka were recorded discussing the timing of
Zuma's prosecution on numerous counts of corruption. The intention of the manipulation was clearly to derail Zuma's chances of
becoming ANC president at Polokwane. Some within the NPA felt
that the recordings indicated that this manipulation 'tainted' the
legal proceedings and amounted to an 'abuse' of the legal process.
For this reason, the NPA decided not to continue with the prosecution, and Zuma was free to contest the 2009 general election
and become the next president of South Africa.

The telephone recordings came to be known as the 'spy tapes'. It
emerged later that they had been made by the National Intelligence Agency (NIA), a state institution. The million-dollar question
that still intrigues people today is how Zuma's legal representatives managed to lay their hands on the transcript of the recordings. Had Zuma infiltrated the intelligence services under Mbeki's
administration to the point where he could easily access the information that would be used to drop the charges against him?
When the NPA made its decision not to prosecute Zuma, the
contents of the recordings they relied upon were still secret. In
challenging the NPA's decision to rely on the recordings in letting
Zuma off the hook, the opposition Democratic Alliance (DA) peti-
tioned the court to demand that the spy tapes be made available
to the party as part of the process of reviewing the NPA decision.[3]

Therefore, the last hurdle that Zuma had to clear before he

---

3   Corruption Watch, 'Spy Tapes Saga: The Latest', 22 August 2013. Available
    at www.corruptionwatch.org.za. Accessed on 20 June 2016.

became president of South Africa was to gain access to a secret recording made by intelligence agents. Once the NPA dropped the charges, Zuma would spend the largest part of his two terms as president fighting all attempts to reinstate the charges against him. His first line of defence was to ensure that the spy tapes were not made public; in that way, the recorded conversations could not be used in any review of whether the decision to drop the charges against him was rational or not. The spy tapes saga was kept alive by the DA for years until the Supreme Court of Appeal ruled in 2014 that the NPA had to comply with a previous court order to hand over the transcripts of the tapes.[4]

While Zuma's access to the secret recordings gave him a political lifeline, the president's relationship with secret information goes way back. After the spy tapes saga emerged, observers and historians focused the spotlight on how entrenched Zuma has been within the intelligence community. For a man outside government institutions – remember, he had been fired as deputy president in 2005 – to be able to access secret recordings belonging to the NIA is frankly baffling. It is possible that access came from someone within the state intelligence apparatus unhappy with Mbeki's attempt to derail Zuma's political career. Controversial former police crime intelligence head Richard Mdluli's name has been mentioned in this regard, with some people believing he could have handed the transcripts of the spy tapes to Zuma's lawyer, Michael Hulley.[5] It was speculated widely in 2007 that Mbeki had a direct hand in Zuma's legal troubles, including the attempts to

---

4   *Destiny*, 'DA wins access to "Spy Tapes"', 28 August 2014. Available at www. destinyconnect.com. Accessed on 3 August 2016.
5   Stephen Grootes, 'Op-Ed: Richard Mdluli returns', Daily Maverick, 6 July 2015. Available at www.dailymaverick.co.za. Accessed on 17 August 2016.

prosecute him for corruption.[6] Therefore it is possible that Zuma may have had sympathisers within the state intelligence services at this time. If that is the case, it is important to explain the basis of their support.

The answer to these questions might lie in the fact that Zuma has had a long-term connection to the intelligence community, and he also knows how it operates. This could explain how he pulled it off. All he had to do was to go back to his notes as the chief of MK intelligence and reactivate some of his old allies in government. Perhaps Zuma has always had a parallel intelligence network that was stronger than that of the state. During his years in exile, Jacob Zuma headed the much-feared iMbokodo, responsible for counter-intelligence within the exiled ANC.

According to journalist Patrick Laurence, iMbokodo was inclined 'to assume that intellectual independence and lack of servility were the tell-tale signs of the presence of enemy agents intent on undermining and destroying the ANC'.[7] The notoriety of iMbokodo, writes Laurence, led to a rebellion within the ANC camps in Angola in 1984. Among the issues linked to Zuma's role in the ANC's counter-intelligence body was the case of Thami Zulu, an MK commander who was detained by iMbokodo in 1988, only to die a within a week after being released by the unit, in 1989.[8]

Reflection upon the activities of ANC members in exile camps is one way to understand how the party would regard independent thinking within its ranks and in society in general when in govern-

---

6   Andrew Feinstein, 'Mbeki's hand clearly evident in Zuma's troubles over the years', 22 December 2007. Available at www.allafrica.com. Accessed on 10 May 2015.
7   Patrick Laurence, 'Jacob Zuma and iMbokodo', politicsweb, 3 March 2009. Available at www.politicsweb.co.za. Accessed on 20 August 2016.
8   *Ibid.*

ment. If influential members of the ANC have a history of paranoia and an inclination to believe in conspiracies, it is more than
likely that such views will inform their attitudes in government.
Throughout his presidency, Zuma's conduct and statements have
revealed his paranoia and reliance on intelligence information
to remain a step ahead of his detractors, and he is all too ready to
believe that people have ulterior motives in what they say and do
in public.

The president seems to have held the view that Public Protector
Thuli Mdonsela, EFF leader Julius Malema, former DA parliamentary leader Lindiwe Mazibuko and Amcu leader Joseph Mathunjwa
were agents working for the US Central Intelligence Agency (CIA).
If Zuma did not believe this, he would not have allowed the State
Security department to go ahead and issue a statement in March
2015 that they needed to 'verify' the allegations that these individuals were linked to the CIA.[9] When I interviewed Zuma in
March 2015, I asked the president if he could go on record about
whether there was an investigation into the Public Protector's
alleged links to foreign spies. The president stated he could not go
on record about the matter because there 'might be a judicial
inquiry'.[10]

A month after my conversation with Zuma, I raised the same
issue with the then Public Protector during an interview at her
office in Pretoria. Madonsela said she was worried about the possible investigation, stating that she had no links whatsoever with
foreign spies and was only doing her job. She mentioned, however,
that no one from government had officially informed her about a

9   Stephen Grootes, 'Thuli Madonsela: State Security Agency lied to the nation',
    Daily Maverick, 17 March 2015. Available at www.dailymaverick.co.za.
    Accessed on 8 August 2016.
10 Interview with Jacob Zuma, March 2015.

possible investigation, and only 'one journalist' had mentioned it to her. Peddling information and not committing to that information in public are typical spy tactics. The allegation that the Public Protector was a spy could have been meant to unsettle her, to isolate her and to weaken trust in her office. Whether or not this was a deliberate strategy on the part of the government, which was facing disparaging reports from the Public Protector's office, is another issue. The troubling trend is that Zuma is willing to entertain the idea of conspiracies, and even to threaten to commit state resources to test the credibility of such allegations.

Shortly after Zuma took office in 2009, he focused his attention on the intelligence services, with the newly appointed Intelligence minister, Siyabonga Cwele, announcing a major overhaul of the Intelligence department. Cwele stated that a large part of the Intelligence budget was spent on corporate affairs, such as communications and liaison, instead of on the 'collection' of information, which is a core mandate of the department.[11] The focus would shift to the collection of intelligence information, taking the department back to its main area of focus. To show that Zuma prioritised intelligence, Cwele would soon fire three intelligence agency bosses for transgressions that involved investigation into 'state capture' by the influential Gupta family,[12] among others. Cwele dismissed NIA chief Gibson Njenje, his foreign intelligence counterpart, Mo Shaik, the head of the South African Secret Service, and Jeff Maqetuka, director-general of the State Security Agency.

Zuma laid bare his obsession with hiding information when

---

11 Leon Engelbrecht, 'Cwele announces a major intelligence overhaul', Defence-Web, 5 October 2009. Available at www.defenceweb.co.za. Accessed on 2 August 2016.
12 Carien du Plessis, 'Ex-spy bosses to spill beans on Guptas', *Mail & Guardian*, 24 March 2016. Available at mg.co.za. Accessed on 28 June 2016.

the Protection of State Information Bill, widely known as the 'Secrecy Bill', was introduced during his tenure. The intention of the Bill, which was proposed and tabled in parliament in 2011, was to limit access and possession of certain information held by the state. The possession and publication of such information would become an offence, which could result in the imposition of a jail term.[13] The state has considerable leverage in deciding what information should not be in the hands of citizens. Civil society organisations and the media campaigned against the bill, which was passed by parliament and was, at the time of writing this, still waiting on the president's desk to be signed into law. The position of civil society organisations is that, if the bill were to be implemented as law, it would be illegal for journalists to be in possession of information such as the expenditure on the Nkandla project. In effect, this could mean that reporting on matters such as Nkandla could lead to imprisonment.[14]

With visibly increasing levels of corruption, the main concern was that Zuma's government would use the process of classifying information to hide information from the people. It would be impossible under such conditions for journalists to carry out certain types of investigative work. Issues such as Nkandla and the impending nuclear deal would remain rumours, with no tangible information showing what has happened. This is the type of democracy that some ANC leaders seemingly find appropriate. However, they get very irritable when asked to explain how their tactic

13 Nelson Mandela Foundation, 'What is still wrong with the Protection of State Information Bill?', 10 October 2013. Available at www.nelsonmandela. org. Accessed on 2 August 2015.

14 Open Democracy Advisory Centre (ODAC), 'Implications of Nkandla Report for the Secrecy Bill', 2013. Available at www.opendemocracy.org.za. Accessed on 3 August 2016.

differs from similar measures enacted under the apartheid system, which thrived on secrecy and 'dark' intelligence information.
If this Bill is signed into law, Zuma could use it to classify the
Nkandla project as 'top secret' in an effort to remove it from
public discourse.

A major feature of the Zuma presidency has been the prominence of the Justice, Crime Prevention and Security (JCPS) ministerial cluster. Most of Zuma's blunders have had to be mopped up
by the ministers from this cluster, which includes the departments
of Police, Defence and Military Veterans, State Security, Justice
and Correctional Services, and Home Affairs. What has brought
all these departments together under Zuma's administration is that
they all contribute various levels of secret information or intelligence about the country.

When the Gupta family's private aircraft landed at the Water-
kloof Air Force Base on 30 April 2013, it was the ministers from
the JCPS cluster who were called in to clean up the mess and to
carry out an investigation into the matter.[15] Government's investigation and position on Nkandla also came through the security
cluster.[16] When students marched to parliament during the 'Fees
Must Fall' campaign, the Minister of Higher Education and Training, Blade Nzimande, went to address the students, but was 'flanked
by ministers from the security cluster'.[17] I thought it would have

15 South African Government, 'JCPS Ministers on report of investigating team
   examining landing of chartered commercial aircraft at Air Force Base Water-
   kloof on 30 April 2013', 19 May 2013. Available at www.gcis.gov.za. Accessed
   on 3 August 2016.
16 News24, 'Security cluster submits Nkandla response', 15 November 2015.
   Available at www.news24.com. Accessed on 2 August 2016.
17 Bekezela Phakathi, 'Students storm gates of parliament in "fees must fall" protest against budget', *Business Day*, 21 October 2015. Available at www.bdlive.
   co.za. Accessed on 30 August 2016.

been more appropriate for Nzimande to be accompanied by the Minister of Science and Technology, and maybe the Minister of Social Development. I did not see any reason for the security cluster to be involved in an education issue in the first place.

The wall that has been built around Zuma by the security cluster ministers is an indication that the president sees many problems as being security-based in nature. Often, the excuse from government is that beneath most public unrest lies the work of foreign agents, who intend to destabilise the country. The funny part of this analysis is that once the state declares that a problem has security implications, then the government concludes that it has no obligation to explain the details further, because there are supposedly security implications if they reveal any details to the public. It's a merry-go-around, and in most cases the government is clueless about what is actually happening.

Securitising socio-economic problems is the oldest trick in the book, and the quickest way to block open debate on issues that need to be aired publicly. Perhaps Zuma's political survival has nothing to do with his reliance on intelligence information; perhaps there is no strategy, and here we are searching for complex, hidden explanations. If indeed Zuma has survived all these years because he relies on intelligence in government, why is it that in most cases his intelligence people fail to detect the events that shake South Africa? For instance, the killing of 34 mineworkers by police at Marikana on 16 August 2012[18] suggests that the intelligence services failed to alert the authorities, which might have averted the tragedy. The burning of more than 20 schools in

18 South Africa History Online, 'Marikana Massacre 16 August 2012', 21 June 2016. Available at www.sahistory.org.za. Accessed on 12 August 2016.

Vuwani,[19] in Limpopo province, after communities rejected the decision of the municipal demarcation board, also caught intelligence officials off-guard. Even more recently, the burning of property in Tshwane, following the ANC's decision to nominate Thoko Didiza as mayoral candidate in the 2016 local government elections, also raised concerns about the capacity of the intelligence agencies to detect threats.

Clearly Zuma loves his intelligence buddies, and he likes to be seen with them as he attends to every new crisis in the country. There are, however, serious questions about the effectiveness of the intelligence services in government. They have been found wanting on several occasions. Of course, there might be major things that they have prevented, but what could be more important than preventing the Marikana massacre? Or could it be that the intelligence services are so busy protecting Zuma and his ANC allies against local political enemies that they do not have the time or capacity to source information to protect the state and all South Africans against real threats? The ANC's internal battle for leadership has become increasingly nasty, with leaders utilising state resources to fight factional battles within the party. From the spy tapes, we know the political abuse of intelligence agencies was a reality under the Mbeki administration, but clearly it has intensified during the Zuma years.

In the search for what has sustained Zuma's hold on power over the years, it is important not to make the common mistake of overlooking the obvious: patronage politics within the ANC. The role of the intelligence agencies in his survival is limited, in my view, and the performance of the intelligence community has

---

19 News24, 'Vuwani on lockdown as more schools torched', 5 May 2016. Available at www.news24.com. Accessed on 3 August 2016.

been amateurish at best. This does not mean, though, that Zuma believes in the power of intelligence. He could be a one-man intelligence team, responsible for the collection, analysis and classification of information that he needs to make sure he is always a step ahead of everyone. There is no doubt that Zuma has been a step ahead since the day he set foot in the Union Buildings – perhaps even before then.

What eludes many people about Zuma is why he has had no match within the ANC. Someone who is able to get rid of him. Maybe, when Zuma goes, we will see how simple his methods really were. Now that would be the work of a master spy. There is a saying that goes, if you want to hide something, keep it in plain sight.

ELEVEN

Zuma's ANC has lost it

After nearly eight years as president of the country, Jacob Zuma has given us sufficient material to judge whether or not he has been a good president. After one term in office, it usually becomes clear whether a president has a clue about what needs to be done, or whether he is still figuring out how to accomplish the basics. The first term gives an indication as to where things are going. This is when the president outlines his plans and sets some of these into motion. The first term is also a good probationary period. Quite often, the election for a second term is to a certain extent a referendum on whether the first term proved that the leader has some form of vision.

In the 2009 elections, the ANC under Zuma's leadership attained 65.9 per cent of the votes countrywide. That was a resounding mandate, an indication that the president and his party had been given an opportunity to implement their policies.[1] In the 2014 elections, the party secured 62.1 per cent.[2] Before the 2014 elections, Zuma said he was aiming for a two-thirds majority,[3] which

---

1   'Election Resources: Republic of South Africa' (online). Available at www. electionresources.org.za. Accessed on 3 August 2016.
2   'Electoral Commission of South Africa' (online). Available at www.elections.org.za. Accessed on 20 June 2016.
3   Ranjeni Munusamy, 'Gigaba takes the ANC elections wheel as Zuma aims for two-thirds win', Daily Maverick, 30 September 2013. Available at www. dailymaverick.co.za. Accessed on 10 July 2016.

he stated would allow the ANC to 'change laws'. Zuma failed to attain this goal. In fact, the 2014 elections showed a slight dip in the ANC's electoral performance.

Under the leadership of Thabo Mbeki, between 1999 and 2008, the party's electoral support grew by 7.1%. Mbeki had inherited a solid party, and he increased its support steadily. Jacob Zuma, on the other hand, has presided over a decline in support of 7.3 per cent in the two national elections in which he has led the party. I am not going to touch on the ANC's performance in local government elections, because in those elections councillors play a big role in leading campaigns and securing votes. When it comes to national elections, however, a large part of the party's success rests on the shoulders of the party leader and his or her track record.

Of course a party's success at the ballot box does not *only* rely on a party leader. There are many different factors that have an impact. The ANC's poor performance in elections under Zuma's leadership has something to do with the divided party that he inherited from Mbeki. Perhaps also the political system is maturing, and the ANC's landslide electoral victories will become a thing of the past as the party is evaluated against its performance in government.

Yet this does not fully explain how the ANC assesses its leaders. Why did the party remove Mbeki so hastily when the party's electoral performance had improved under his leadership? The same party seemingly sees nothing wrong with a president who has not only cost the party votes, but has also became a public relations nightmare because of the scandals surrounding him.

Looking at the numbers, it seems almost bizarre that the ANC is so incapable of evaluating Zuma's leadership critically. Instead of asking searching questions about where he seems to be leading the party and the country, immense efforts have been channelled towards defending him. The ANC seems not to be perturbed by its declining electoral support. We should ask, therefore, if there is any achievement that might redeem Zuma, something that would enable the party to regain the ground lost in terms of electoral support. Let's look at the economy first.

When Thabo Mbeki left office in 2008, South Africa's gross domestic product (GDP) was growing at 3.2 per cent. GDP measures growth of the economy in terms of what the country produces by adding value to products and services. Economists sometimes argue about the meaning of GDP, but in its simple sense it is a measure of economic activity based on what people earn and how they spend.[4] A lower GDP means there is less economic activity in the country, and that the economy is simply not growing. When Zuma took over as the president in 2009, annual economic growth measured in terms of GDP was sitting at – 1.5 per cent. This means that the economy was not growing; it was actually shrinking.

During Mbeki's tenure as president, the economy grew at an average of 4 per cent year on year.[5] The average rate of economic growth since Zuma took over in 2009 has been 1.7 per cent. The only way for Zuma to take the economy to an average of 4 per cent during the remainder of his tenure is for the economy to grow by 18 per cent for the next two years. Not even China has achieved this kind of growth.

This does not at all make for a good economic story to tell. Zuma and his Cabinet ministers often use the global economic slowdown as an excuse for South Africa's low economic growth,

---

4   Investopedia, 'What is GDP and why it is so important to economists and investors', 25 March 2015. Available at www.investopedia.com. Accessed on 5 August 2016.
5   The World Bank, 'GDP growth (annual %)'. Available at data.worldbank. org. Accessed on 10 May 2016.

but the main problem with the economy under Zuma is not external factors such as the global recession. The problem is Zuma's talent for wrecking the economy.[6] Of course the global recession has had a negative impact, but the Zuma government could have and should have acted to minimise the effect. Instead it worsened the impact.

Economic growth in 2015 was dismal, measuring less than 1 per cent. I often ask people what they think needs to be done in order to grow the economy at a rate of 1 per cent per annum. I ask this question because, in my view, a government does not need to do much to grow an economy by 1 per cent. If the economy of a country like South Africa were simply left alone, without any proper leadership, I believe it would probably grow on its own by at least 1 per cent per annum.

The problem emerges when Zuma gets his hands on the economy and makes disastrous decisions, such as replacing Nhlanhla Nene with Des van Rooyen as Minister of Finance. The Public Investment Corporation (PIC), the state investment arm, has admitted to parliament that it lost R99 billion of the value of its holdings within 48 hours of that move.[7] Nevertheless Zuma and the ANC still maintain that the president's decision was not the real cause of the losses.

In his parliamentary reply to the opposition DA's question regarding the wiping out of billions of rands in shareholder value as a result of his decision, Zuma blamed 'speculative attack'[8] on

---

6   Songezo Zibi, 'Zuma's economy-wrecking legacy', *Business Day*, 14 December 2015. Available at www.bdlive.co.za. Accessed on 14 April 2016.
7   Gaye Davis, 'DA seeks answers following PIC's billion rands loss', Eyewitness News, 11 May 2016. Available at ewn.co.za. Accessed on 30 July 2016.
8   Gaye Davis, 'Nenegate wasn't sole cause of PIC's R99bn loss, insists Zuma', Eyewitness News, 14 July 2016. Available at ewn.co.za. Accessed on 30 July 2016.

the economy. In Zuma's view, opportunistic investors and stock market hyenas took advantage of his well-intended decision by selling off stocks and deliberately causing the losses. I suppose these must be the same people who are behind the lower levels of economic growth that have characterised Zuma's tenure in office. They were brought out of retirement to undermine Zuma when he took over in 2009. Those economic hyenas, the speculators, were nowhere to be seen when the country was averaging 4 per cent GDP growth under Thabo Mbeki. This explanation makes Zuma the chief excuse-maker when it comes to the country's poor economic performance. He talks big projects, yet those projects seem to be aimed at lining the pockets of certain people instead of taking South Africa forward.

There are many key areas in which the government has an opportunity to create jobs. Public procurement, for instance, can be utilised very effectively to create jobs. When the government undertakes projects to build schools and other public infrastructure programmes, the opportunity arises to create jobs. But the government's massive expenditure in the public service has not produced this outcome. The tender system does not contribute much when it comes to job creation. This is because those who win tenders to provide services in government are not asked to do so in a way that provides job opportunities. People who are employed under the public works programme are often exploited, because the fat cats who win the tenders seek the maximum profit. Hiring many people to do the job and paying them decent salaries are not part of the equation.

The rot that has consumed the South African Broadcasting Corporation (SABC) under Zuma is another great cause for concern. The SABC has been reduced to a conduit of patronage and cronyism. Under chief operating officer Hlaudi Motsoeneng, so-called sunshine journalism has become the highest form of patriotism.[9] Motsoeneng is understood to have a direct line to Zuma, and flaunts his access as he tramples on the editorial independence of the national broadcaster. The Public Protector's investigation into the SABC revealed the collapse of corporate governance, yet the government is unable (or unwilling) to correct the situation.[10]

The ANC as a party has been publicly embarrassed by how Zuma's cronies at the SABC publicly ignore the party. Cronies such as Motsoeneng seemingly report to 'Ubaba' (father) Zuma and not to the ANC. Minister of Communications Faith Muthambi, who is supposed to implement ANC policy, has seemingly cut ties with the party. Muthambi has become belligerent and ignores the party's policy position, the position that needs to be implemented in government and also at the SABC. Things have deteriorated so badly that the ANC chief whip, Jackson Mthembu, had to step in, pleading for SABC to stop embarrassing the party and to respect editorial independence.[11] The SABC's decision not to air footage of public protests was declared by the Independent Communications Authority of South Africa (Icasa) to be invalid and in contravention of the provisions for free media in country.[12]

Zuma has used the party to build a strong network of patronage for himself. He has done this so well that the party's internal

9   Ranjeni Munusamy, 'Why Hlaudi and the league of "untouchables" remain bullet proof', Daily Maverick, 13 July 2016. Available at www.dailymaverick.co.za. Accessed on 3 August 2016.

10 Carien du Plessis and Matuma Letsoalo, 'SABC blatantly ignores public protector's report', Mail & Guardian, 18 March 2016. Available at mg.co.za. Accessed on 10 June 2016.

11 Business Day, 'ANC's Jackson Mthembu lays into Hlaudi Motsoeneng', 5 July 2016. Available at www.bdlive.co.za. Accessed on 3 August 2016.

12 Katharine Child, 'SABC ban on protest coverage illegal, Icasa finds', TimesLive, 11 July 2016. Available at www.timeslive.co.za. Accessed on 1 August 2016.

processes have been severely weakened. The state of the ANC is such that a chief operating officer at the SABC, who didn't even pass matric, can stand tall and say that the party is misleading the people when it asserts that the SABC was wrong to ban footage of public protests.[13] The ANC has lost it, and the party has to stand by and watch as Zuma tightens his grip on power, to the disadvantage of the party.

Another area where Zuma has cemented his hold, and is consolidating it further, is with the state-owned entities. Institutions such as South African Airways (SAA), Transnet and Eskom are all targeted for control and influence. These institutions control billions of rands in public money and are among the biggest spenders, because they provide critical services for the country. Under Zuma's administration, however, SAA has become a vehicle for dispensing patronage.[14] The once-proud national carrier has been embroiled in financial mismanagement under its Zuma-aligned board chair, Dudu Miyeni. Miyeni is one of the untouchables in government, and National Treasury officials know this. Before he was fired, Finance minister Nhlanhla Nene had begun to ask tough questions about the financial implications of some of the decisions taken by the SAA board, and particularly by Miyeni. Nene was shown the door, and Miyeni triumphed. This was no coincidence.

In a situation where the economy is simply not growing, good governance and a focused policy stance when it comes to state-owned entities could actually save the day. If managed properly, state-owned entities such as SAA could be used as targets to

---

13 Natasha Marrian, 'No one will tell the SABC what to do, says Hlaudi Motsoeneng after ruling', *Business Day*, 11 July 2016. Available at www.bdlive. co.za. Accessed on 3 August 2016.

14 *Business Day*, 'SAA peddles fallacy on BEE', 1 December 2015. Available at www.bdlive.co.za. Accessed on 3 August 2016.

rejuvenate the ailing economy. This is where government spends its money wisely, and pursues some of the policy goals that would otherwise be difficult to pursue through the private sector. Electricity generator Eskom has become another conduit of corruption, as tenders to provide coal for power stations are increasingly awarded to politically connected individuals and companies.[15] This has grown to a point where it affects mining rights. The 'Zupta family' (a mocking reference to the alliance of financial interests between the Zuma family and the Gupta family) now has a firm hold on Eskom.[16]

Further, some of these deals involve some of Zuma's children, who have made major inroads into business since their father became president. The explanation by Zuma's defenders is that his children should be allowed to enter into business partnerships just like any other South African. This explanation does not see anything wrong with the children of high-profile politicians doing business with government. Even the ANC secretary-general, Gwede Mantashe, sees nothing wrong with politically connected families doing deals with government.[17]

The problem with this new breed of entrepreneur is that they gobble up just about any business opportunity in front of them, and they are working fast. They have a stake in mining, production companies for soap operas, supplying uranium for the yet-to-be-built nuclear plants, and so forth. These people work at a fast pace

15 Carol Paton, 'Eskom "overpays" Guptas for coal', *Business Day*, 14 June 2016. Available at www.bdlive.co.za. Accessed on 30 August 2016.

16 *City Press* and Fin24, 'Eskom contract helps "turn Gupta, Zuma coal mine around"', 12 June 2016. Available at www.fin24.com. Accessed on 30 August 2016.

17 Natasha Marrian, 'Mantashe defends Zuma daughter's appointment', *Business Day*, 29 July 2014. Available at www.bdlive.co.za. Accessed on 30 August 2016.

because they know that once their parents or grandparents are no longer in power, their business opportunities might run dry.

And there are also questions about South Africa's foreign policy on the African continent. Granted, not everyone is as focused on the continent as was Thabo Mbeki, who championed the African Renaissance dream along with his counterpart, President Olusegun Obasanjo of Nigeria. The idea of the African Peer Review Mechanism (APRM), which was introduced under Mbeki, focused on assessing progress among African states in relation to good governance, financial management and economic growth. In 2006, I participated in the process of drafting South Africa's self-assessment report. We focused on how South Africa was performing when it came to things like the rule of law, accountability in government and government responsiveness.

South Africa was a champion of the APRM initiative, and Mbeki's supporters prioritised it. At one point during the drafting process, we spent nearly all night deliberating with government officials about how to report on the threat South Africa was facing from money laundering and other illicit flows. The APRM had the potential to assist African countries in learning from each other in a safe space where they set the rules on how to assess each other. It was through the APRM that South Africa's foreign policy on the continent was beginning to take shape. I did not agree with the manner in which the Mbeki administration retained control of the process, often muzzling the voices of civil society organisations. However, the initiative was sound, and was pursued with gusto.

Alas, when Jacob Zuma took over, the APRM took a back seat. South Africa's agenda on the continent became muddled by crude self-interest, and the government's foreign policy became more and more mysterious. In 2010, barely a year after Zuma took over, his nephew Khulubuse Zuma walked away with a 'lucrative oil deal' in the troubled Democratic Republic of Congo (DRC).[18] He has made significant inroads in business since his uncle set foot in the Union Buildings. The relationship between Jacob Zuma and DRC president Joseph Kabila has been the subject of speculation as to whether it is a bilateral business relationship, a diplomatic one, or both. Kabila has used his close relationship with Pretoria to hold on to power in the DRC, even delaying elections in the country.[19] Zuma's compromising business interests in the DRC, in the form of mining concessions,[20] undermine South Africa's diplomatic leadership on the continent. The issues relating to Kabila's hold on power in the DRC may be more complicated than the way they are generally presented; however, Zuma's diplomatic intervention lacks credibility because it is seen as a pursuit of self-interest. This does not help the situation.

Since 1994, South Africa has become known as a country that greatly values freedom, democracy, transparency and the protection of human rights. South Africa's story of democracy has been an inspiration for many countries on the continent. However, lately, other tales are told. In 2015, when I travelled to Addis Ababa, Ethiopia, people would ask me: 'How big is Zuma's Nkandla palace?' This was after the EFF had been hammering at the issue in parliament for more than a year. Clearly, the Nkandla scandal has made waves beyond our borders, and this has great implications for Zuma, the ANC and South Africa's reputation. With Zuma's

---

18 amaBhungane, 'Zuma Inc's DRC oil coup', *Mail & Guardian*, 30 June 2010. Available at mg.co.za. Accessed on 30 August 2016.

19 Carien du Plessis, 'Congolese point accusing fingers at Zuma and Dlamini-Zuma', *Mail & Guardian*, 17 May 2016. Available at mg.co.za. Accessed on 20 June 2016.

20 *City Press*, 'Jacob Zuma's family empire', 27 July 2014. Available at www.news24.com. Accessed on 2 August 2016.

administration lurching from one scandal to another, South Africa can no longer be taken seriously on the continent as a country that can advise on democracy. Against this background, it is difficult for South Africa to convince fellow African countries to respect their parliaments and ensure that their governments account to the people. Of course it is not the role of South Africa to police the continent, but it is important to acknowledge that South Africa can no longer be said to lead by example and is to be taken seriously on issues relating to accountability and good governance.

Corruption scandals have plagued Zuma's second term as president. But reports of corruption emerged during his first term, and even before he became the president of the party in December 2007. Allegations of corruption featured strongly in the trial of his former financial advisor, Schabir Shaik, as far back as 2001. His defenders would counter that all the evidence that has emerged raising concerns about Zuma's judgement is indicative of a wider conspiracy to discredit him. This is a wholesale defence, where everything is lumped together as anti-Zuma paranoia.

For now, it seems Zuma is immune from the political effects of all the scandals surrounding him. Trying to judge him on his performance when it comes to growing the economy is pointless. He has no sense of accountability, and would plead ignorance on things he ought to have known as a leader. The reality, however, is that none of those problems are regarded by the ANC as grounds to recall Zuma. Elsewhere on the planet, political leaders do not survive even minor scandals, or political decisions that turn out to be mistaken, but Zuma is seemingly untouchable.

Following the 'Panama Papers' leak in 2016, the prime minister of Iceland resigned from office after his name featured on the list of wealthy individuals who have money stashed in offshore tax havens.[21] Africans in general, and South Africans in particular, might have thought the Icelandic people were crazy, that they were vandalising democracy, by removing the prime minister on the basis of such a small issue. Here in South Africa, however, a finding by the Constitutional Court that the president failed to uphold the Constitution, the highest law in the land, is not grounds for his removal.[22] British prime minister David Cameron also resigned in 2016, after the people of Britain voted in a referendum to leave the European Union (EU).[23] Cameron had supported the position that Britain should remain within the EU. When the results of the referendum came in, the prime minister realised that he no longer enjoyed the mandate of the people and he resigned. He clearly believed he could not carry on leading the British people, as they had rejected his position on so-called Brexit. Such a move would be unthinkable in our situation, where leaders believe they are anointed to lead the nation.

There are many reasons why Zuma should have left office by now. There is a litany of scandals and bad decisions, especially his failure to uphold the Constitution, which should have had Zuma reflecting deeply as to whether he still has enough credibility to lead South Africa. If Zuma was unable to realise on his own that he ought to resign, then the ANC as a party should have served as another layer through which Zuma's conduct in office could be

21 BBC News, 'Panama Papers: Iceland PM Sigmundur Gunnslaugsson steps down', 6 April 2016. Available at www.bbc.com. Accessed on 30 August 2016.

22 Jessica Elgot, 'Jacob Zuma breached constitution over home upgrades, South African court rules', *The Guardian*, 31 March 2016. Available at www.theguardian.com. Accessed on 30 August 2016.

23 *The Guardian*, 'David Cameron resigns after UK votes to leave the European Union', 24 June 2016. Available at www.theguardian.com. Accessed on 30 August 2016.

evaluated. A sober decision should have been made to ask him to leave. Instead of the party taking a tough position on Zuma, the party asked the people to forgive him for his poor judgement on the Nkandla matter.[24]

What would it take for Zuma to leave office? Some have speculated that the ANC has a plan B to remove Zuma sometime after the 2016 local government elections.[25] The problem with the idea of a plan B is the presumption that Zuma is still ANC president because the ANC still wants him there. It requires us to believe that the ANC will suddenly wake up and decide to remove him, and that Zuma is sitting somewhere wringing his hands and waiting for the ANC to decide his fate. This is not the case at all. The very idea of publicising plan B in the newspapers is because those who are behind it are merely testing the waters. They can say all they want outside the ANC; within the ANC, there is only one man in charge and that is Jacob Gedleyihlekisa Zuma, Ubaba! I do not think Zuma has any interest in some half-baked plan B, especially when he is at an advanced stage of setting up his own exit.

24 Dineo Bendile and Ziyanda Ngcobo, 'ANC's branches reaffirm decision to accept Zuma's apology on Nkandla', Eyewitness News, 31 May 2016. Available at ewn.co.za. Accessed on 30 August 2016.
25 Business Tech, 'The ANC's plan B to get Zuma out', 3 April 2016. Available at www.businesstech.co.za. Accessed on 31 August 2016.

TWELVE

When Zuma goes

Some might think that when Zuma goes, the scandals and rot that have plagued the country under his leadership will disappear with him. It is tempting to think that, once he leaves, an automatic reset button will be pushed and the country will return to its pre-Zuma state. Hopefuls might even believe that when Zuma goes, a new ANC leadership will arise that truly puts the country first. Under this new leadership, corruption, patronage and nepotism will no longer be tolerated, the economy will regain momentum, and slowly but surely things will look brighter for all South Africans. If you are very optimistic, you might believe the tension between the government and the judiciary will subside, because the government will choose to respect the rule of law even when it does not suit them.

The unfortunate reality, however, is that Zuma's eventual departure will not mean an end to our troubles. There is no reset button. It is impossible to return to a pre-Zuma South Africa. Even if Zuma falls, the damage he has done will remain for a long time to come. His successor faces the formidable task of cleaning up the mess. The Zuma years have been a rough ride.

There are positive and negative consequences of Zuma's presidency. The negative aspects are obvious: high levels of unemployment, poor economic growth, confusion over South Africa's foreign policy, corruption and high levels of crime. Amid all this, there is a surprising up side: Zuma has taught South Africans the valuable lesson never to trust leaders blindly. Leaders should be held accountable, because if they are trusted blindly some leaders will use their power to enrich themselves instead of serving their country and its people. It takes a very long time for some nations to learn this lesson. In some countries, people believe that their leaders can do no wrong.

Right across our northern border is Zimbabwe, where the majority of the population once believed that Robert Mugabe was their saviour. Instead, Mugabe is responsible for running the country's economy into the ground. Today in Zimbabwe, some people ask: why was Mugabe entrusted with Zimbabwe in the first place? Didn't we see him for what he really was, or did he change along the way? What gave Mugabe power to extend his hold on power was that a sizeable part of the population believed everything he said and could see no reason to doubt his intentions. When he extended his administration and entrenched his personal power, no one raised doubts about the man and his long-term plan for Zimbabwe. Mugabe become bolder and bolder, taking over Zimbabwe and running it like a personal fiefdom. By the time he resorted to violence and intimidation to hold on to power, including rigging elections, it was too late; he was already entrenched in the system. He had created a system of rule by the few and powerful.

The people of Zimbabwe had no opportunity to be taught not to trust leaders blindly, especially those who see themselves as anointed to lead. South Africans, on the other hand, have been shown the reasons why they should question leaders and hold them to account. Openly questioning politicians and demanding transparency are the best ways to ensure accountability in government. Zuma has shown South Africans why they should not trust politicians blindly. The Nkandla issue and the allegations of state capture by the rich and powerful have provided a clear lesson: do not trust leaders/politicians, no matter how much you may adore them as people. The main question is whether South Africans will heed this lesson, or whether they will see the experience of Zuma's leadership as a once-off experience. Were South Africans even awake throughout Zuma's disastrous tenure, or was Mandela's nation fast asleep, dreaming about the great nation the world once thought them to be?

All nations make wrong turns once in a while. The United States had George W Bush, who plunged the country into the war in Iraq in 2003, on the pretext that Saddam Hussein possessed weapons of mass destruction. The decision was a grand miscalculation; no weapons of mass destruction were found.[1] Bush's years as president left the country deeper in debt and embroiled in unwinnable wars.[2] British prime minister Tony Blair supported Bush in the doomed Iraq expedition, dragging his country into an unnecessary war. Looking at the leadership provided by these leaders and the bad decisions they made, there is little doubt that their respective nations made wrong turns by electing them as leaders. What distinguishes nations from each other, however, is what they learn from their wrong turns and how soon they return to the right path.

Equally, South Africa can be forgiven for taking a wrong turn. But it is important to ask whether South Africa has learned anything from this experience. South Africa can survive Zuma, but it is uncertain whether the nation will not repeat the same mistake in the future. The process of returning to common sense depends on

---

1   Associated Press, 'CIA's Final Report: No WMD found in Iraq', NBC News, 25 April 2005. Available at www.nbcnews.com. Accessed on 17 July 2016.
2   Henry Blodget, 'The truth about who's responsible for our massive budget deficit', Business Insider, 11 July 2011. Available at www.businessinsider.com. Accessed on 17 July 2016.

the lessons learned. The simple lesson that has been delivered by Zuma is that the nation should not stop questioning politicians, including the seemingly good ones. Whoever leads the country should always be kept on their toes. They should know that active citizens are watching them, and that they cannot do whatever they want and expect to get away with it. Good politicians who work for the people do not mind when people question their motives because they know that is how they are held accountable. That is the kind of politician who knows that trust is not given; it is earned. Therefore, if people express concerns about a leader, it is the duty of that leader not to spend time accusing citizens of working for foreign interests or of being CIA spies, but to work towards earning their trust, and thus removing their doubts.

A true leader does not see it as a personal attack when asked to explain his motives. An honest leader takes up the opportunity to tell their side of the story and builds trust through transparency. A dishonest politician declares war immediately when asked to explain his motive. To be treated with doubt is something that is loathed by a crooked leader; he realises that explaining himself will not help the situation. He then vows to fight fire with fire, and teach his enemies a lesson. He declares that his enemies never gave him an opportunity in the first place. That he was asked to explain his motives is not seen as an opportunity to earn trust; he sees that as a way to set him up to prove his idiocy.

Under Zuma, there have been more robust and open engagements about the future of the country. In my discussions with people in the media and the private sector, there is desperation to understand where the country is headed. I often tell them that the answer depends on the position and perspective of the person asking the question.

Someone from the private sector might be wondering: what will happen to business if the African National Congress (ANC) goes down under Zuma? Will the Economic Freedom Fighters (EFF) take over and nationalise the mines? What will happen to property rights? Will the private sector be able to attract foreign investors? Will the EFF ruin the trust of foreign investor in the country's economy? These questions show the level of uncertainty within the private sector about the future. If the risk management captains in the private sector cannot figure out where things are going, then we have a major problem. Doubts and uncertainty have assailed our country as never before. Before 1994, the greatest uncertainty was whether South Africa would succeed in becoming a democratic country without turning into a bloodbath. But our democracy is airborne; the problem is that it is encountering ferocious headwinds under Zuma.

As a fragile nation, we are struggling to make sense of the level of uncertainty and doubts about the direction of our country. For the private sector, it is of utmost importance to lessen the level of uncertainty, so as to predict what the future holds. As far as business is concerned, the policy implementation environment has been stifled under Zuma, and there are too many contenders who could actually influence policy direction. The idea that a particular family could influence Cabinet appointments[3] would certainly raise doubts about the stability and predictability of policy positions in such a configuration. The ANC is also resuscitating its populist rhetoric to ensure that people do not start believing the EFF drafted the Freedom Charter. The main problem is that growing populist rhetoric has begun to shape the behaviour of political parties.

---

3   Emma Graham-Harrison, 'Jacob Zuma denies influence of the wealthy Gupta family in South African Cabinet', *The Guardian*, 17 March 2016. Available at www.guardian.com. Accessed on 2 August 2016.

Everyone wants transformation of everything as early as next week. The careful nuances that have shaped this debate in the past are all gone.

Jacob Zuma's leadership provided a political space that was seized by parties such as the EFF to justify why they came into being. The outcome is that the democratic gains created under Zuma, in the form of a more robust national engagement about leadership, cannot be reversed once he leaves office. The chaos that has become part of opposition politics cannot be reversed. The manner in which the EFF relates to parliament is something that will continue for a while – either through the EFF or another opposition party, including those to come. At the end of the day, Zuma's leadership and the manner in which he has dealt with his political enemies – including through the use of state institutions – is something that will for a long time form part of South African politics.

There is nothing exceptional about what is happening in South Africa when we compare it to the evolution of postcolonial states on the continent. The only difference is that in South Africa there is in principle a commitment to constitutional democracy. There are institutions such as the Public Protector and the Human Rights Commission responsible for safeguarding our constitutional democracy. The Constitution also provides the principle of the separation of powers, to ensure 'checks and balances' in exercising power. This principle is important because it serves as a powerful framework through which the system can self-correct, as seen with the Constitutional Court ruling on the Nkandla matter. What is even more interesting about South Africa is that the system is highly decentralised, something that goes against the instincts of the ANC. It means that there are many institutions responsible for protecting democracy. It is difficult for a single person, or an interest group, to capture the entire state. One can capture some institutions, for example the police or the National Prosecuting Authority; however the courts and the Chapter 9 institutions will (hopefully) remain intact and will be able to keep democracy on its feet. The Chapter 9 institutions, which include the Public Protector, the South African Human Rights Commission (SAHRC) and the Auditor-General, are mandated in the Constitution to protect democracy. It was through the proper functioning of the Public Protector that South Africans came to understand why the president had no right to benefit unduly from the security installations to his private residence at Nkandla.

It is possible that a particular interest group might manage to capture and control a department, such as the National Treasury, or the Department of Trade and Industry, to pursue their narrow interests. However, it is difficult to imagine interest groups being able to bring all departments, or the entire bureaucracy, under control at the same time. This is a great benefit of the decentralisation of state and government institutions; it protects the institutions from being captured all at once. It also requires a high level of co-ordination to utilise the capture to pursue the goals identified by the culprits. Zuma's struggle with the Treasury and other institutions of the state is an indication that full state capture under democracy is difficult to achieve; we can even discuss how clumsy his project of trying to capture the state has become.

As a governing party, the ANC has yet to master how to actually configure the bureaucracy – the various government departments – towards a single goal. The ANC does not like decentralisation because it poses a challenge when it comes to driving the bureaucracy towards a single goal. The party is also frustrated by the division of government into local, provincial and national spheres. As the ANC grapples to hold on to power, the party will be tempted to entertain centralisation as a way to retain its grip on state institutions. For Zuma, centralisation would mean retaining more control of institutions and therefore making sure his plan to procure what he wants is well coordinated from one place. For the ANC, centralisation of power means better control of policy machinery and the implementation of policy. There has even been talk about merging provinces and reducing their numbers, though this has been a subject of discussion since the Mbeki era.[4] Decentralisation spreads accountability of government across many institutions, ensuring that misconduct can be tracked one way or another, which of course is a good thing in a democracy.

Just over 20 years into the democratic era, there is an emerging trend to question the legitimacy of decisions made by the governing ANC. This has intensified under Zuma. The ANC is struggling to make decisions and to ensure that those decisions are followed and implemented in the form of policy. According to political science, governments should have the privilege and legitimacy to make decisions and have those decisions implemented.[5] The central question is: who governs? According to the sociologist Max Weber, people follow decisions that are legitimate. Despite winning elections by resounding majorities, the ANC government under Zuma has experienced a crisis of legitimacy, and the credibility of the party has received a serious knock. The challenge of credibility will continue when Zuma is gone. It is a question of authority. Zuma has vandalised the exercise of authority to a point where people have lost trust in the idea of legitimate authority, even beyond the ANC.

4   Business Tech, 'ANC wants fewer provinces in SA', 21 September 2015. Available at www.businesstech.co.za. Accessed on 12 June 2016.
5   N Jayapalan, *Comprehensive modern political analysis*. New Delhi: Atlantic Publishers, 2002.

An emerging trend is that when the ANC makes a policy decision and seeks to implement that policy, there is a challenge by the trade unions, or by the opposition parties. There is also an emerging trend to challenge authority, even on matters where it is clear that the government is not at fault. But, under Zuma, the government has been at fault too often within a short space of time. The government has lost numerous court cases, where its decisions have been challenged successfully.

The pension reform law and the imposition of e-tolling, as we have seen, are two examples of declining legitimacy. In the case of the pension reform law, criticism from Cosatu and opposition parties challenged the ANC government to a point where it decided to hold back on the implementation of the policy. With e-tolling, the majority of motorists in Gauteng have refused to comply with the law and simply continue to use the road without paying for it. This is an act of open civil disobedience,[6] but stems partly from the decline in legitimacy of the ANC to make and implement difficult policy decisions.

Indications are that South Africa might soon face 'tax revolt',[7] as the educated middle class raises concerns about government's authority to collect revenue amid reported wastage in the public service. The rising levels of corruption, and the increasing public awareness regarding this, would certainly stifle the policy implementation environment. For government to implement policy, it requires legitimacy to make tough decisions, including coming up with the means to collect revenue. It should not require the threat of force for government to collect revenue; citizens should feel compelled to pay their dues.

---

6 Angelique Serrao, 'Why e-tolling will fail – Outa', Independent Online, 3 March 2014. Available at www.iol.co.za. Accessed on 10 June 2016.
7 Solly Moeng, 'Tax revolt threat: heed the signs', Fin24, 6 January 2016. Available at www.fin24.com. Accessed on 3 August 2016.

This is arguably the first time in more than 20 years that we are seeing this type of response to a policy decision. South Africans are beginning to realise that the heritage of the ANC, the party that supposedly freed the people from apartheid, is not enough for the party to remain credible and to have the muscle to implement its policies. The ANC has to govern well and change South Africa for the better to keep its credibility in the long run.

While Mbeki's views on HIV/Aids were problematic, he did not have a general legitimacy or credibility problem. However, Jacob Zuma had a legitimacy problem from day one, because of the corruption charges against him. From the beginning of Zuma's first term, the ANC focused on defending their controversial leader instead of focusing on the implementation of the party's policy decisions. Zuma's links to dubious business people were just the beginning of a presidency that will be remembered mainly for its countless scandals.

Despite Zuma's legitimacy problem, the ANC has continued to defend him over the years. The defence is not really based on whether what Zuma does is defensible or not. No matter what he does, the ANC has stayed loyal to him, fending off his critics at every turn. The private sector and the middle class, two of Zuma's greatest critics, have become the enemies of the ANC, despite the party's repeated claims that poverty and unemployment are the real foes. The reality is that when the ANC feels under pressure, it usually criticises the private sector for being uncooperative in addressing pressing national questions, such as poverty, unemployment and inequality, and attacks the ungrateful black middle class for having betrayed the ANC. The line-up of excuses also includes the Constitution, for being a stumbling block towards full transformation, and the counter-revolutionary media, for failing to tell good stories.

There is very little trust left between the ANC and the private sector. After Nenegate, the ANC defended Zuma for his stance, and suggested that the party was being sabotaged by the private sector.[8] Is this argument valid or not? For me it doesn't matter; what matters is that this position allows the party to survive and manage to explain itself and retain the relationship with its ordinary constituency. The private sector doesn't have any real responsibility toward ordinary people; their priority is their shareholders. In this way, the ANC wins the war of rhetoric, a necessary principle when it comes to dealing with the masses.

If the ANC were seen as having a cordial relationship with the private sector, then the party would be providing ammunition for the EFF to attack them. The EFF seeks to expose any relationship that the ANC might attempt to build with the private sector. The policy position of the EFF is infested with conspiracy theories, that the ANC has no intentions to transform the country because the party has from the beginning surrendered to 'white capital'.[9] For the ANC to prove that this is not the case, the party has to resort to populist policies and language. This leaves the private sector to fend for itself.

One of the (few) gains from Zuma's leadership is the manner in which it has opened the space for engagement about the future of the country. This had not happened until now. Zuma necessitated open engagement about the direction of the country. His leadership also emphasised just how important it is to have a free and independent media that reports without fear or favour. Would

---

8   Business Tech, 'Zuma: don't blame me for Nenegate', 14 July 2016. Available at www.businesstech.co.za. Accessed on 2 August 2016.

9   Ranjeni Munusamy, 'Pursuing the revolution versus "selling out": did the ANC make the right choice?', Daily Maverick, 8 December 2015. Available at www.dailymaverick.co.za. Accessed on 16 July 2016.

we have known the extent of the Nkandla scandal if the media that stumbled upon it had not investigated the matter and reported on it week after week? It was also laid bare under Zuma's leadership that institutions of democracy such as the courts and the Public Protector have the potential to stop the rot in government, if left to operate independently.

The ANC often states that the party is convinced the country has a strong and vibrant democracy, and that the courts can make their decisions independently without fear of government's reaction. But when it comes down to it, there are those in the ANC who are not fully committed to these ideals; they are only committed when they stand to be direct beneficiaries of the decisions of the courts. When decisions do not go their way, they are willing to attack the institutions of democracy and question their mandate in society. These are the people who do not see the importance of ensuring that the space for open, robust discussion that was inspired by the disastrous Zuma years remains open even after he is gone.

Those who do not believe in open, robust engagement would argue that there is no need to continue to view the government's conduct with suspicion once Zuma is gone. They will attempt to write off Zuma's disastrous presidency as a once-off event that will never be repeated. The ANC has one of at least two options of what to do once Zuma is out of office. They can rally and build a strong sense of unity, repelling all criticism. By dealing with internal divisions, the ANC can regain control of its branches and ensure that a new leader does not plunge the party into more scandal. This option would mean that the ANC would have to close the space of robust engagement created under Zuma. This option will not be to the benefit of all South Africans. A misguided shift towards party unity could close debate and discussions within the party, and ultimately in the country.

The other option for the ANC is to learn to exist within the newly created space for open engagement in society. Instead of making evangelical statements such as the ANC is anointed to rule[10] or the ANC will rule until Jesus returns,[11] the party could train its spokespersons to respond to the real issues on the ground and reflect exactly what the party leadership is struggling with. Within the party there must be a space for engagement, and comrades should express their differences on how better to run the country. A democratic ANC with robust internal engagement is a good step towards fostering further democratisation in the country. A united ANC in denial of what is happening on the ground is dangerous. That is the kind of ANC that will begin to shape the society towards the party's fantasy that all is well on the ground. That would be the road to serfdom, paved with unity, pursuit of the national question and silence towards the leaders.

South Africa's democracy is resilient, and the people of this nation have put up with much in the past, including the brutal apartheid regime. Having endured Zuma's leadership, South Africans should at least walk away with lessons for the future, lessons that will ensure they do not veer too far from common sense again.

---

10 Aphiwe Deklerk, 'God chose the ANC to lead', TimesLive, 18 July 2016. Available at www.timeslive.co.za. Accessed on 18 July 2016.
11 Karabo Ngoepe, 'Zuma repeats that ANC will rule until Jesus comes', News24, 5 July 2016. Available at mg.co.za. Accessed on 5 July 2016.

THIRTEEN

After Zuma

At some point, Jacob Zuma will have to vacate the positions of president of the African National Congress (ANC) and president of South Africa. Zuma's tenure as the president of the country officially comes to an end in 2019. South Africa will hold general elections in that year, which will ring in the sixth parliament since 1994. The Constitution states: 'No person may hold office as President for more than two terms.'[1] This unequivocally means that Zuma cannot be the president of the country after 2019. There is a finish line, and he cannot go beyond it.

The question is whether he will get to the finish line, or whether he will be pushed aside or even quit before that point. If Zuma leaves office before the 2019 general elections, how will he go? These are some of the possibilities that carry different assumptions about what is happening within the ANC. Of course one cannot pronounce with certainty as to what is likely to happen. As the former British prime minister Harold Wilson used to say, 'A week is a long time in politics.' But there are things that are unlikely to happen. One thing is certain: Zuma will not just fold his arms and wait for people to decide how he departs. He has survived too long for that. If it comes to him being forced out of office, he would certainly fight back, and he would rather negotiate a dignified exit

---

1   Constitution of the Republic of South Africa, Act 108 of 1996, Section 88(2).

than wait for people to script his departure. He is highly unlikely to leave in the same way as Mbeki did. If it were possible for Zuma to be kicked out of office in the same manner as Mbeki, it would have already happened. Zuma has lived through conspiracies within and outside the ANC, to a point where he must be used to being plotted against.

Before one can speculate how Zuma will go, it is important to acknowledge that he has survived numerous scandals, including Nkandla and the ruling by the Constitutional Court that he failed to uphold the Constitution. If that did not bring Zuma down, then what would? There is something else that needs to be acknowledged about Zuma's tenure in office. It is clear that no one among Zuma's enemies within the ANC can credibly be said to be engineering a plan to ensure his exit or downfall. If there is any group of people within the party who could be said to be working on Zuma's exit, it would be his allies, in the sense of managing his exit for one of their own. If his allies within the party, such as the so-called Premier League – the faction grouped around the premiers of Mpumalanga, North West and the Free State – have their way, which is highly likely, Zuma will leave office when his term in government comes to an end in 2019. This will give space for a successor from the allied camp to settle in.

As for Zuma's enemies within the ANC, they have been at work to remove him since he was elected to lead the party at Polokwane in 2007. That was clear in the intensity of the December 2012 ANC elective conference in Mangaung, during which Zuma triumphed amid a divided party. I attended that conference as part of the media contingent. Many people expected Zuma to be removed as president of the ANC. Not only did that scenario not materialise, but Zuma also cemented his hold on power by winning

75 per cent of the vote[2] and packing the national executive committee (NEC) with his allies. The result of the Mangaung conference was a clear demonstration that Zuma's detractors within the party have not prepared the ground in their quest to have him removed. The same group then complained that Zuma's scandals were ruining the party's reputation. The ANC provincial structure in Gauteng has led the anti-Zuma pack since before the Mangaung conference, and openly supported former president Kgalema Motlanthe to replace Zuma as the leader of the party.[3]

It is therefore important to note that those who have been critical of Zuma as leader of the party have failed to remove him, despite his scandal-ridden tenure in government. One could conclude, then, that scandals alone are not sufficient ammunition to get rid of Zuma. Scandals are only speed bumps for Zuma, minor irritants that occur once in a while. The year 2016 brought intensified calls for Zuma to leave office, a campaign that brought civil society organisations and the opposition parties into a working alliance. The calls gathered force as a result of the Constitutional Court ruling that he failed to uphold the Constitution, the decision by the Pretoria High Court that corruption charges against him should be reinstated,[4] and pressure over the ANC's dramatic loss of support in the local government elections held on 3 August. These are the materials upon which the anti-Zuma forces make their case that Zuma ought to leave office.

2   Ranjeni Munusamy, 'Zuma wins second term', Independent Online, 18 December 2012. Available at www.iol.co.za. Accessed on 3 August 2016.

3   Stephen Grootes, 'ANC winner in Mangaung may still lack legitimacy', Business Day, 19 November 2012. Available at www.bdlive.co.za. Accessed on 19 May 2016.

4   Agence France-Presse, 'South African court rules Jacob Zuma can be charged over corruption', The Guardian, 24 June 2016. Available at www.theguardian.com. Accessed on 20 July 2016.

The question of the reinstatement of corruption charges against Zuma will need to be finalised by the Constitutional Court. If the Court upholds the decision that Zuma should face corruption charges, it will be an interesting development that could have direct implications on the remaining years or even months of Zuma's presidency. The mere possibility that he could face corruption charges has serious implications for how he leaves office. How Zuma goes will also depend on who is set to take over from him. If he has to face corruption charges, this will mean that the president will finally have his day(s) in court. If the Constitutional Court makes the determination that he should face corruption charges before the 2017 elective conference of the ANC, Zuma will certainly do everything in his power to ensure that the incoming president of the ANC is someone who can keep the National Prosecuting Authority (NPA) under his thumb and make sure they do not prosecute him.

Suppose the Court says the prosecution has to go ahead; there is still a possibility that Zuma will get off the hook. This is possible if the NPA goes to court with the aim of bungling the case, or even misplaces the docket. Zuma could skate free on the pretext that prosecutors are unable to prove that he is guilty of corruption. Given the NPA's insistence thus far that there is no reason to prosecute Zuma, it is clear that the NPA will be a reluctant prosecutor in this case. If that happens, then either the opposition parties or civil society organisations may pursue a private prosecution. There are already those who are expressing frustration with the state's reluctance to prosecute cases that implicate connected politicians. Popo Molefe, board chair of the Passenger Rail Agency of South Africa (Prasa), has drawn attention to the apparent reluctance of the police and the NPA to prosecute alleged corruption relating to financial maladministration at the state-owned entity.[5] Molefe expressed frustration at how the internal battle within the ANC impacts upon decisions to prosecute corruption in the country. He claims that politicians are meddling with investigations and prosecutions. For this reason, he is threatening to go the private prosecution route.

A private prosecution of Zuma could mean that the retired president would still need to have influence on his successor within the ANC, to ensure that the state continues to thwart any attempt to prosecute him.

The possibility of having to answer to corruption charges is one of the compelling reasons why it is of crucial importance for Zuma to make sure the 'right person' is his successor. Another reason why he would need to continue to have influence on his successor is to ensure that no one rapidly unpicks the patronage network that he will surely leave behind. The last thing an outgoing president needs is for his successor to begin investigating decisions that were made in the past, particularly questionable ones such as those relating to the influence of the Gupta family in state-owned entities such as Eskom. This is a real risk for Zuma.

Zuma's current hold on the law enforcement authorities does not guarantee that they would not turn against him in once he is gone. There would be no incentive for law enforcement and prosecution authorities to keep on punting Zuma's position if he is no longer president. However, if Zuma's successor comes through his loyalist camp within the ANC, then that would provide a reprieve for the outgoing president.

The uncertainty regarding what will happen with the corruption allegations against Zuma must be the biggest risk factor he

---

5   Pauli van Wyk, 'ANC "riff-raff" fingered in Prasa scandal', *Mail & Guardian*, 15 July 2016. Available at mg.co.za. Accessed on 19 July 2016.

has had to confront in his political career. He has fought this case throughout his presidency, and the case seems to be nearing its conclusion as his presidency comes to an end. I am convinced that if the Constitutional Court makes the unlikely ruling that the NPA was within its rights to halt Zuma's prosecution in 2009, then the opposition parties will start a process of private prosecution. Even if the NPA feels it cannot prosecute, because of the political meddling with the case in 2007 (as supposedly revealed by the spy tapes), this does not mean that in essence Zuma cannot be prosecuted. The cloud of corruption surrounding Jacob Zuma provides much political mileage for the opposition parties; hence they are unlikely to let the case rest anytime soon. Even after Zuma is gone, the ANC will be constantly reminded of how it doggedly defended a man who had no regard for the Constitution and the laws of the country.

There have been attempts by some within the ANC to give the impression that a plan was being drawn up for Zuma to leave office in the final months of 2016. This is improbable. After the March 2016 Constitutional Court judgment that Zuma had failed to uphold the Constitution, reports began to surface in the newspapers stating 'ANC top brass plan Zuma exit'.[6] The essence of the claim was that Zuma is willing to leave office before the end of his term in 2019. Some of the people working on the plan confirmed to the media – anonymously, of course – that Zuma was 'willing to step down to save the image of the ANC'. This is strange, for while these reports were emerging, Zuma's supporters were out defending him, saying that he had not actually violated the Constitution, he had only failed to uphold it. My sense of the matter is that the only people within the ANC who could have

---

6   Matuma Letsoalo, 'ANC top brass plans Zuma exit', *Mail & Guardian*, 31 May 2016. Available at mg.co.za. Accessed on 19 July 2016.

power and influence to negotiate Zuma's exit are his allies, and specifically the Premier League, made up of Free State premier Ace Magashule, North West premier Supra Mahumapelo and Mpumalanga premier David Mabuza. If indeed his allies were working on a plan, they would not punt it in the media. The fact that the existence of this plan surfaced in the media is to me an indication that it did not come from Zuma's corner. This further shows that those who are working on the plan are not at the centre of power within the ANC; hence they try to ensure that what they have in mind gains traction in the ANC and across society by stating through the media that the plan exists. I suspect that there was no such plan, and the media reports were an attempt by these individuals to test the waters and see how such a plan would be received.

It also seems unlikely that Zuma, who has fought fiercely to stay in power, would suddenly put the interests of the country first and let the 'top brass' work out how and when he ought to leave office. This is improbable, given the overwhelming evidence that Zuma's faction within the ANC has been piling up one victory over another. For Zuma to allow his fate to be decided by people who do not come from his corner within the ANC, the president would have to be severely weakened. There is no proof that Zuma has been weakened significantly. He has actually been more daring than before, like a man who is about to complete his mission and will stop at nothing to do so. Among his daring moves was the decision to fire Finance minister Nhlanhla Nene in December 2015. Zuma has also defied the ANC – or his detractors within the party – through his continued support of Hlaudi Motsoeneng's reign of terror at the South African Broadcasting Corporation (SABC).[7]

---

7   Ferial Haffajee, 'Hlaudi's reign of terror – Jimmy Mathews speaks', *City Press*, 3 July 2016. Available at city-press.news24.com. Accessed on 20 July 2016.

In mid-2016, Motsoeneng instituted an editorial policy that the public broadcaster would not broadcast footage of violent protests on TV. This policy, according to Motsoeneng, is an indication of responsible journalism. For Motsoeneng, who is transparent about his alliance with Zuma, people should not see public acts of violence on television, as it undermines the government.[8] Even the ANC's secretary-general, Gwede Mantashe, and the party's chief whip in parliament, Jackson Mthembu, stated that they found the SABC's editorial position indefensible and embarrassing.[9] The two have openly criticised the SABC, but Zuma has remained quiet about the matter. Motsoeneng hit back saying that 'no one will tell the SABC what to do'[10] – not even the governing party with a mandate to implement policy. It is only the courts that have a record of stopping Zuma and his allies; the ANC as a party has not been able to do that.

There are clearly divisions within the ANC over what to do about the Zuma situation. Much was made in 2016 of the idea that the local government elections would be a referendum on Zuma's leadership.[11] Thus, if the ANC performed badly in the elections, then that would justify a move to recall Zuma immediately afterward. But this theory has many holes. Why would a drop in electoral support amount to a compelling case to kick Zuma

8   Mpho Raborife, 'Zuma using Motsoeneng to turn SABC into state broadcaster – Maimane', News24, 27 June 2016. Available at www.news24.com. Accessed on 3 August 2016.

9   Stephen Grootes, 'ANC's Mthembu hits back at SABC board chair', Eyewitness News, 7 July 2017. Available at ewn.co.za. Accessed on 3 August 2016.

10 Natasha Marrian, 'No one will tell the SABC what to do, says Hlaudi Motsoeneng after Icasa ruling', TimesLive, 11 July 2016. Available at www.timeslive.co.za. Accessed on 19 July 2016.

11 Allister Sparks, 'Local government elections: a referendum on Zuma', Business Day, 20 July 2016. Available at www.rdm.co.za. Accessed on 19 July 2016.

out as ANC president, if even the Constitutional Court judgment on Nkandla was not enough to get rid of him? The reality is that it is up to the ANC to decide whether or not they want to blame Zuma. No matter how bad the results of any election, Zuma's influential supporters within the party can always go back to the party branches and explain that the problem is 'white capital' or the media failing to report the ANC's 'good story to tell'. Clearly for the ANC, poor performance in local government elections on its own was never going to make a compelling case for removal. Zuma can only be removed if there is an overwhelming unity within the ANC, especially within the National Executive Committee, against him.

Zuma's removal before the 2017 ANC elective conference is a step that would advantage his detractors, and would certainly not work well for his allies. His allies need him to take them straight into the 2017 elective conference, to set the ball rolling for the emergence of their preferred candidate. Therefore, the idea that Zuma's removal after the local government elections would save the party's reputation was never satisfactory, and was not shared by Zuma's allies. This idea would be seen merely as ruse by Zuma's detractors, a tactic to get a step ahead for the 2017 elective conference of the party. This scenario does not add up, unless Zuma is really tired of continuing and he volunteers to leave.

There is, however, a possibility that Zuma could leave after the 2017 elective conference of the party. If he leaves after 2017, without being recalled, no one can claim victory for his departure. After all, the president is elderly and has had health issues over the years. If his preferred candidate takes over in 2017, Zuma will probably have a say in whether he carries on as president of the country for another year or retires early. There would be no reason for him to carry on if his preferred candidate is in charge. Zuma could graciously step down, and use that moment to say that, for him, it never was about holding on to power.

Of course there is the very important question of who will likely succeed Zuma. This is a difficult and nearly impossible question to answer. Even if one could provide an educated guess, what is more important is the balance of power within the ANC, and how the new leader would emerge through that configuration. Various names have been put forward as possible successors. The natural successor in terms of how things stand within the party would be Cyril Ramaphosa, the current deputy president of the ANC.

Ramaphosa rose to the second most powerful position in the ANC during the Mangaung battle between Zuma, who was seeking a second term as the leader of the party, and his then deputy, Kgalema Motlanthe, who was contesting Zuma's position. Zuma's supporters and allies within the party opted for Ramaphosa to become Zuma's deputy, and Motlanthe was defeated. Ramaphosa's position can therefore be seen as a vote against Motlanthe rather than as a vote for Ramaphosa. Since then, there has been speculation that Ramaphosa was there for a short while and would be ditched at the 2017 elective conference. As far back as 2013, it was rumoured that Ramaphosa would not be allowed to progress to the helm of the party.[12] His success in becoming the deputy president of the ANC was merely to ensure that Kgalema Motlanthe was sidelined.

It is highly unlikely that Ramaphosa will rise to the number-one position in the party as easily as he became the deputy president. If he seriously starts mobilising support soon, Ramaphosa could

12 George Matlala, Mogomotsi Magome and Candice Bailey, 'Plot to dump Ramaphosa', *Sunday Independent*, 21 July 2013. Available at www.iol.co.za. Accessed on 19 July 2016.

stand a good chance of becoming the president of the party. But as someone who has observed his tenure thus far, I feel that Ramaphosa has struggled to build his own support base within the party. He has sung Zuma's praises in government, and once in a while says something cryptic about good governance. It seems to be a challenge for Ramaphosa to become his own man and take a strong position on issues of governance.

With the rating agencies breathing down South Africa's neck, Ramaphosa could be seen as the saviour for the ailing economy. As a businessman, Ramaphosa is not a denialist when it comes to the impact of inflation. He would assist South Africa in getting back onto a sound economic path. The problem is that ANC branches do not vote on the basis of such things as the ability of a candidate to grow the economy. They usually vote on the basis of factions that exist within the party. Ironically, the fact that the business community in South Africa and abroad have shown confidence in Ramaphosa's leadership could become a problem for him within the party. The question asked in a *New York Times* headline, 'Could Cyril Ramaphosa Be the Best Leader South Africa Has Not Yet Had?',[13] is one of those international accolades that could cost one the ANC presidency. If Ramaphosa means business in terms of the quest to lead the ANC, he needs to adjust his strategy to fit ANC politics; he will have to fight fire with fire. Otherwise, he will certainly lose the battle for the ANC's top position.

Another candidate who has been placed in the frame is Zuma's ex-wife, Nkosasana Dlamini-Zuma. She served as a Cabinet minister under Mandela (as Minister of Health), Mbeki (as Minister

---

13 Bill Keller, 'Could Cyril Ramaphosa Be the Best Leader South Africa Has Not Yet Had?', *The New York Times*, 23 January 2013. Available at www.nyt.com. Accessed on 19 July 2016.

of Foreign Affairs) and Zuma (as Minister of Home Affairs), re-
spectively, and was elected to the chair of the African Union (AU)
in 2012. Dlamini-Zuma's putative candidacy might gain traction
from the call by the ANC Women's League that the time for a
woman president has come.

After five years at the helm of the AU, Dlamini-Zuma decided
not to run for a second term. This signals her availability for the
leadership contest within the party. While Dlamini-Zuma has, at
the time of writing this book, not yet stated explicitly that she
is available to run for the ANC presidency in 2017, she has not
denied it either. The problem with Dlamini-Zuma's candidacy is
that it is seen as a way to ensure that Cyril Ramaphosa does not
become the president of the party. The call for a woman president,
it has been argued, is to ensure that Cyril Ramaphosa does not
succeed Zuma. It has been a tradition within the party that the
deputy succeeds the president.[14] In all fairness, tradition within
the ANC is a thing of the past. In 2007, as the deputy president
of the party, Jacob Zuma ran against Thabo Mbeki, who was seeking a third term. Zuma has said that he would never stand for a
third term as ANC president, and I don't believe he will change
his position.[15] Zuma might not need to stand for a third term in
order to remain influential within the party and the country beyond his official tenure as the president of the party. He can achieve
that by ensuring that his proxy becomes the president of the party
and of the country.

Being a Zuma by marriage, Dlamini-Zuma's candidacy could
be seen as an extension of the Zuma hold on power. Given that

14 *The Weekly*, 'Choosing Zuma's successor', 15 January 2016. Available at www.
theweekly.co.za. Accessed on 18 July 2016.

15 Qaanitah Hunter, 'Zuma: I will never stand for a third term', *Mail & Guardian*, 10 October 2015. Available at mg.co.za. Accessed on 3 August 2016.

she would need the blessing of an incumbent to succeed, Dlamini-Zuma faces a difficult challenge. The Zuma name has become a liability, and some people within the ANC may not want another Zuma in office.

There is always a chance that a dark horse could emerge as the leader of the ANC in the 2017 party conference. It is also not impossible that Ramaphosa and Dlamini-Zuma could team up, with Ramaphosa as the president and Dlamini-Zuma as the deputy. This arrangement could mean the healing of divisions within the ANC – at least temporarily – and moving beyond the factionalism that has characterised the party in recent years. This would be a conciliatory picture. However, the depth of divisions within the party, and the way this has been institutionalised in the form of patronage and corruption, may not allow for a conciliatory picture to emerge. This would require members of the ANC to work together and ensure the party is saved from capture by interest groups. This would also require the different camps within the ANC to realise that they are weaker when they are divided. This position, though, may be difficult to achieve, and would require more work to be done to deliver the ANC beyond the Zuma years.

The Zuma years show an entrenched structure characterised by deep levels of patronage. This structure dates back to the Mbeki years, but it has been perfected under Zuma. As long as the solutions for South Africa's problems are understood to be located within the ANC, it will take the ANC to 'self-correct' before the necessary changes can trickle down to affect the country positively. It also means that the country will have to wait for the self-correction process to get underway within the ANC. The waiting may be too long, and there is no guarantee that the ANC has what it takes to self-correct. Perhaps the very idea is just a myth, a nostalgic harking back to the history of a party that was once a truly great liberation movement.

Epilogue

The main question I have sought to answer in this book is: how do we understand the various political shifts that have taken place under the administration of President Jacob Zuma? These are shifts that will, I believe, continue to have an impact on the African National Congress (ANC) even after Zuma is gone. Zuma is a product of the ANC, and he has made efforts to shape the ANC in a way that guarantees his political survival. He represents a system, a particular way of doing things. Zuma has shaped the relationship between the ANC as a ruling party and the people of South Africa. Other political opportunities have presented themselves because Zuma was in charge; I refer to these as the remnants of Zuma's leadership. The idea that when Zuma leaves office some of those remnants of his leadership will cease to exist is merely a pipe dream.

Zuma's leadership has created the space for a new type of opposition, and it has sustained that opposition to a point where ordinary South Africans are beginning to pay attention. For example, the politics of disruption pursued by the Economic Freedom Fighters (EFF) has gained momentum and relevance during Zuma's tenure. Disruption will continue to be pursued as a means to attain political goals, even when Zuma is gone. This way of bargaining for political goals casts doubt on the effectiveness of formal political engagement as a way to take society forward. Illegal land occupation, for example, has become a swifter and more efficient way to answer calls by the dispossessed to achieve justice than has patient and careful adherence to rules and procedures.

Under Zuma's leadership, the institutions of democracy in South Africa have suffered a decline in legitimacy. The Zuma system flouts the law, and shows a disregard for the Constitution, thereby putting democracy at risk. These problems can be resolved if a credible leader emerges within the ANC to strengthen democracy. However, it takes hard work and a great deal of effort to restore the credibility of democratic institutions once they are damaged. If democracy is vandalised, as has been the case under Zuma, ordinary people become prey to populist sentiments propagating simplistic solutions. If a political party uses its majority in parliament to push through indefensible positions, such as blindly defending Zuma on the enormous expenditure on his private residence at Nkandla, then people will start asking whether democracy is indeed the best political tool to correct the ills in a society. The damage caused by this will take years to correct, despite the existence of an independent judiciary capable of fearlessly pronouncing on wrongdoing by government and other stakeholders in society.

There are ways of testing democracy that society should rather avoid. One of those ways is to keep resorting to the courts for answers to questions of maladministration. Democratic societies should function in a way that those who are involved in maladministration and corruption do not have to wait for a court ruling before apologising for wrongdoing. It should be downright uncomfortable for wrongdoers to use the public space to defend themselves when they are caught out. Citizens should hold political parties to the highest moral standard, and parties should not provide platforms for those who have wronged communities.

The system that has been put in place during Zuma's tenure in office thus far has generated a toxic narrative that says those who complain against corruption and maladministration are simply a minority influenced by white interests. The level of patronage and the institutionalisation of corruption are severe, and represent major threats to the legitimacy of democracy.

In understanding the ills of our society, it is tempting to conclude that the problem is Zuma, and that the ANC should resolve the problem by removing him. The problem with this solution is that it assumes that the majority of ANC members are innocent bystanders in all this, and that they are being held to ransom by one man. Zuma has come to power through the ANC, and the party has sustained his hold on power. Zuma has become the system within the ANC, and this system will seek to entrench itself further once Zuma goes. This could mean that Zuma's replacement might perpetuate the same legacy of corruption, albeit in a more cautious way. The scandals might become fewer, while corruption mounts as the system is perfected.

As the ANC battles to become a modern political party capable of leading the state in the right direction, South Africans need to ask themselves if it is wise to locate the solutions to the country's problems within the party. What would it take for the ANC to turn the corner and move away from making itself a vehicle for patronage and corruption? The ANC will not self-correct because it is the right thing to do. Maybe the ANC will wake up when it becomes clear to the party that continuing on the path of self-destruction will eventually cost them everything. At this point, it seems the ANC thinks it can get away with feeding the system of corruption and patronage that has come to define the party under Zuma's leadership. Certainly, there are those within the party who will attempt to benefit from the system of patronage. They might argue: if Zuma, with his enormous credibility problems, could get away with it, why not me? When Zuma goes, everything will not suddenly get better. It might even get worse, unless the nation puts a stop to this, because clearly the ANC won't.

Acknowledgements

This book was partially borne out of discussions I had with Maryna Lamprecht, both as a journalist and subsequently as the commissioning editor for the book. Her guidance has been instrumental throughout the project. I am indebted to her for her patience and foresight.

I would like to thank my editor, Alfred LeMaitre, for patiently working with me in shaping the text. His sharp eye helped to ensure that I covered as much as I could and provided the necessary details to strengthen my points. Thanks also to my incredible researcher, Patience Kelebogile Salane, for filling in gaps in the text. Credit also goes to a good friend, Tom Learmont, for helping me to get the process of writing the book off the ground. Tom has been great in assessing some of my earlier thoughts about South Africa politics.

I am forever indebted to my wife, Margaret, for encouraging me to write and keep on writing. Her feedback on the earlier draft of the manuscript helped me to believe that I just might have a book on my hands.

About the author

RALPH MATHEKGA is one of South Africa's leading political analysts and columnists. He taught politics at the University of the Western Cape and worked as a senior policy analyst at the National Treasury. He is often quoted by both local and international media houses and comments regularly on television and radio. Ralph is currently completing a PhD in politics. He and his wife, Margaret, live in Johannesburg.

Index

～～～